CONSTRUCTION CLAIMS

Adam Constable

and

Calum Lamont

Acknowledgements

Crown copyright material is reproduced with the permission of the Controller of HMSO and the Queen's Printer for Scotland.

Clauses from the ICE Conditions of Contract (7th edition), published by Thomas Telford and the Institution of Civil Engineers, are reproduced with permission.

Clauses from contracts by the Joint Contracts Tribunal Limited, Sweet & Maxwell, © The Joint Contracts Tribunal Limited, are reproduced here with permission.

Clauses from the NEC3 Engineering and Construction Contract are reproduced here with permission from NEC Contracts.

Please note: References to the masculine include, where appropriate, the feminine.

Published by the Royal Institution of Chartered Surveyors (RICS)
Surveyor Court
Westwood Business Park
Coventry CV4 8JE
UK
www.ricsbooks.com

No responsibility for loss occasioned to any person acting or refraining from action as a result of the material included in this publication can be accepted by the authors or RICS.

ISBN 978 1 84219 346 4

© Royal Institution of Chartered Surveyors (RICS) December 2007. Copyright in all or part of this publication rests with RICS, and save by prior consent of RICS, no part or parts shall be reproduced by any means electronic, mechanical, photocopying or otherwise, now known or to be devised.

Typeset in Great Britain by Columns Design Ltd, Reading, Berks

Printed in Great Britain by Page Bros, Milecross Lane, Norwich

Printed on Greencoat Paper – Greencoat is produced using 80% recycled fibre and 20% virgin TCF pulp from sustainable forests.

Contents

Preface vii

List of Acts xi

Table of cases xiii

Introduction xxiii

1 **Payment claims** 1
   1.1 Lump sum contract 1
   1.2 Remeasurement contract 9
   1.3 Prime cost contract 12
   1.4 Quantum meruit 12
   1.5 Payment claims under the Housing Grants, Construction and Regeneration Act 1996 25
      1.5.1 The payment provisions 26
      1.5.2 Withholding notices 27

2 **Certification** 34
   2.1 Certificates or approval as a condition precedent to payment 34
      2.1.1 The JCT conditions 35
      2.1.2 The ICE conditions 36
   2.2 Validity of the certification process 37
   2.3 Can certificates be binding? 42

3 **Variation claims** 44
   3.1 What is a variation? 44
   3.2 Instructions 48
   3.3 Reliance upon information provided by the employer 49
   3.4 Omission of work 51

Contents

	3.5	Conditions precedent to claiming for additional work	53
		3.5.1 The JCT Standard Form of Building Contract with Quantities (2005 edition)	54
		3.5.2 The ICE Form of Contract (7th edition)	56
		3.5.3 The NEC Contract ECC3	58
4	**Time for completion and extensions of time**		**61**
	4.1	Introduction	61
	4.2	'Time for completion'	62
	4.3	Establishing an entitlement to an extension of time	66
	4.4	Standard form contracts	82
		4.4.1 JCT 2005	83
		4.4.2 ICE (7th edition)	97
		4.4.3 NEC3	99
	4.5	Delay and determination – time of the essence	106
	4.6	Concurrent delay	110
	4.7	Ownership of the 'float'	113
		4.7.1 Position under JCT	113
		4.7.2 Position under NEC3	115
5	**Liquidated damages**		**116**
	5.1	Introduction	116
	5.2	The *contra proferentem* rule	117
	5.3	The operable extent of an LAD clause	119
	5.4	The operation of the 'prevention principle'	121
	5.5	Penalty clauses	124
	5.6	Contractual peculiarities	132
		5.6.1 Entries against the appendix	133
		5.6.2 The problem of sectional completion	134
		5.6.3 Contractual preconditions to recovery	136
		5.6.4 Extension of time	138
		5.6.5 Termination	138
		5.6.6 'Waiver'	139
		5.6.7 Standard forms	139

6	Loss and expense claims		147
	6.1	Introduction	147
		6.1.1 Overriding principles of a loss and expense claim	147
	6.2	Contractual formalities	149
	6.3	Standard forms	151
		6.3.1 JCT 2005	151
		6.3.2 NEC3	154
		6.3.3 ICE7	154
	6.4	Heads of loss	156
		6.4.1 Prolongation costs	156
		6.4.2 Increased site overheads	156
		6.4.3 Increased office overheads	158
		6.4.4 Increase in cost of materials	159
		6.4.5 Wasted management time	161
		6.4.6 Disruption costs	165
		6.4.7 Loss of profit	166
		6.4.8 Finance charges	166
		6.4.9 Loss of bonus	167
		6.4.10 Sums paid in settlement of third-party claims	168
		6.4.11 Cost of claim collation	172
		6.4.12 Other losses	179
	6.5	Global claims	179
	6.6	The SCL protocol	183
	6.7	Expert delay/disruption evidence	184
		6.7.1 Delay claims	184
		6.7.2 Disruption claims	186
7	Termination		188
	7.1	Contractual termination	188
		7.1.1 Compliance with notice provisions	188
		7.1.2 Unreasonable or vexation termination	193
		7.1.3 Contractual termination and other existing rights	196

Contents

    7.2   Repudiatory breach of contract   199

Index   203

Preface

This book, like the other titles in the *Case in Point* series, is aimed at chartered surveyors and other professionals working in the construction and property industries.

While chartered surveyors may not need the breadth of knowledge of the law of their opposite numbers in the legal profession, they do need a similar depth of knowledge in those areas of the law which impinge directly on their work. Consequently, there are, for example, plenty of building surveyors who know more about the law relating to party walls, and plenty of quantity surveyors who know more about adjudication, than the average lawyer in general practice.

So surveyors need law, albeit in different specialist areas, according to the nature of their practice. This means that they need to maintain and develop their understanding of the law. The knowledge acquired at college, or in studying for the RICS Assessment of Professional Competence (APC), has a limited shelf life, and needs to be constantly updated to maintain its currency. Even the best practitioners (perhaps especially the best practitioners) are aware of the difficulty of keeping abreast of changes in the law. The most up-to-date specialist needs a source of reference as an aide-memoire or as a first port of call in more detailed research.

The *Case in Point* series

The books in the *Case in Point* series are aimed at construction and other property professionals who need to upgrade or update their legal knowledge, or who need access to a good first reference at the outset of an inquiry (which is how lawyers also sometimes use them).

The series was established as part of the RICS Books commitment to meet the needs of surveying (and other) professionals. It was developed as a response to the particular difficulties created by the burgeoning of reported decisions of the courts. The sheer scale of the law reports, both general and specialist, makes it very hard to identify the significance of a

Preface

particular decision, as part of a wider trend, as an isolated anomaly limited to its facts, or as a landmark departure in the law.

So it was decided to focus on developments in case law, although these are placed where necessary in the context of statutory or standard form contract provisions. In any given matter, the practitioner will want to be directed efficiently to the decision(s) bearing upon the issue with which he or she is dealing; in other words, to 'the case in point'. The authors have been selected as having the level of expertise required to be selective and succinct. The result is a high degree of relevance without sacrificing accessibility. The series has developed incrementally and now forms a collection of specialist handbooks which can deliver what practitioners need – the law on the matter they are handling, when they want it.

Construction Claims by Adam Constable and Calum Lamont

As recently as 50 years ago, construction law was not a major area of legal practice; indeed, it may not have been considered a separate area of law at all. One of the engines of the phenomenal growth of construction litigation, arbitration and most recently adjudication has been the incidence of claims in construction and engineering contracts. Given the large sums of money at stake and the complexity of modern construction projects, the phenomenon of disputes arising from these claims is not surprising, although the scale often is. Major contractors have parts of their organisations devoted to advancing claims, whose preparation may begin almost as soon as construction is underway (cynical observers might say that it can begin even earlier). A whole new occupational group has grown up to represent contractors and clients respectively, and many quantity surveyors in particular describe themselves as claims consultants.

The cases covered in *Construction Claims* bear witness to the size and importance of the claims industry, even though they only represent a tiny fraction of the multitude of claims generated. Their subject matter comprises the familiar battlefields: contractual payment and quantum meruit, including certification procedure, variations and their valuation and other instructions, and time and extension of time, including delay and disruption. The cases provide essential guidance on the stance of the courts in relation to particular types of claim and moreover on the procedural constraints under the contract and rules of civil litigation/arbitration which govern their submission.

Preface

The task of assembling this body of case law and organising it, with statutory and contractual provisions and comment, has required skill and experience of construction disputes.

The authors, Adam Constable and Calum Lamont, are both barristers at Keating Chambers, a leading set in construction-related work.

Adam has more than 11 years' experience of major construction litigation, including a number of appearances in the Court of Appeal; he was appointed as Treasury Counsel in 2004. He publishes frequently in legal and industry journals, and is consistently recommended as a leading construction junior in the legal directories.

Calum was called to the Bar in 2004 and has been a member of Keating Chambers since 2005. He has advised in a number of significant construction, engineering and utilities disputes.

These authors have already produced the successful *Building Defects* title in the *Case in Point* series; Calum Lamont also co-authored *Contract Administration*, with Gideon Scott Holland. *Construction Claims* is a significant addition to the construction law element of the series, which also includes *Construction Adjudication* and *Party Walls*.

Anthony Lavers, 2007
Professional Support Lawyer, White & Case, London
Visiting Professor of Law, Oxford Brookes University
Consultant Editor, Case in Point series

x

List of Acts

The following Acts are referenced in this publication.

Builders Licensing Act 1971 (NSW)
Housing Grants, Construction and Regeneration Act 1996
Limitation Act 1980

The text of this publication is divided into commentary and case summaries. The commentary is enclosed between grey highlighted lines for ease of reference.

Table of cases

Abbey Developments Ltd v PP Brickwork Ltd [2003] CILL 2033 51
Adkin v Brown [2002] NZCA 59 202
Admiral Management Services Ltd v Para-Protect Ltd [2002] 1 WLR 2722 176
Aerospace Publishing Ltd v Thames Water Utilities Ltd (2007) 110 Con LR 1, CA 163
A L Barnes Ltd v Time Talk (UK) Ltd [2003] 1 BLR 331 18
Alfred McAlpine Homes North Ltd v Property and Land Contractors Ltd (1995) 76 BLR 59 .... 157, 159
Amalgamated Building Contractors Ltd v Waltham Holy Cross UDC [1952] 2 All ER 452 68
AMEC Building Ltd v Cadmus Investment Company (1996) 51 Con LR 105 51
AMEC Process & Energy Ltd v Stork Engineers & Contractors BV [2000] BLR 70 .... 177, 180
AMEC Process and Energy Ltd v Stork Engineers & Contractors BV (No. 4) [2002] CILL 1883 176
Appleby v Myers (1867) LR 2 CP 651 2
Architectural Installation Services v James Gibbons Windows (1989) 46 BLR 91 .... 189, 196
Babcock Energy Limited v Lodge Sturtevant Ltd (1994) 41 Con LR 45 161
Bacal Construction (Midlands) Ltd v The Northampton Development Corporation (1975) 8 BLR 88 50
Baese Pty Ltd v R A Bracken Building Pty Ltd (1989) 52 BLR 130 (Australia) 133
Balfour Beatty Building Ltd v Chestermount Properties Ltd (1993) 32 Con LR 139, 62 BLR 1 .... 73, 108
Banque Paribas v Venaglass [1994] CILL 918 22

Table of cases

Case	Page
Bedfordshire County Council v Fitzpatrick [1998] CILL 1440	109
Bell & Son (Paddington) Ltd v CBF Residential Care and Housing Association (1989) 46 BLR 102	136
Bernhard's Rugby Landscapes Ltd v Stockely Park Consortium Ltd (1997) 82 BLR 39	180
Biggin & Co Ltd v Permanite Ltd [1951] 2 KB 314	168
Bilton v Greater London Council (1982) 20 BLR 1	71
Birse Construction Ltd v Co-operative Wholesale Society (1997) 84 BLR 58	40
Bolton v Mahadeva [1972] 1 WLR 1009	2, 173
Bottoms v York Corp (1892) Hudson's BC (4th edn) vol. 2, p. 208; (10th edn) p. 270	45
Bovis Lend Lease v RD Fire Protection (2003) 89 Con LR 169	170
BR & EP Cantrell v Wright & Fuller Ltd [2003] BLR 412	40
Bramall & Ogden Ltd v Sheffield City Council (1983) 29 BLR 73; (1983) 1 Con LR 30	72, 134
Bridge UK.Com Limited v Abbey Pynford plc [2007] CILL 2465	164
British Airways Pensions Trustees Ltd v Sir Robert McAlpine & Sons Ltd (1994) 72 BLR 26	180
British Glanzstoff Manufacturing Co Ltd v General Accident, etc, Ltd [1913] AC 143, HL	138
British Steel Corp v Cleveland Bridge & Engineering (1981) 24 BLR 94; [1984] 1 All ER 504	14, 64
British Thomson-Houston Co v West (1903) 19 TLR 493	137
Bruno Zornow (Builders) Ltd v Beechcroft Developments (1989) 51 BLR 16	135
Buckland v Watts [1970] 1 QB 27	175
Bywaters & Son v Curnick & Co (1905) KB 393, CA	167
C & P Haulage v Middleton [1983] 1 WLR 1461 at 1467, CA	148
Canterbury Pipe Lines Ltd v Christchurch Drainage Board (1979) 16 BLR 76	47
Carlton Contractors v Bexley Corp (1962) 60 LGR 331	48
Cellulose Acetate v Widnes Foundry [1933] AC 20, HL	119
CFW Architects (a firm) v Cowlin Construction Ltd [2006] EWHC 6, TCC	130, 135, 171

Case	Page
Charles Rickards Ltd v Oppenheim [1950] 1 KB 616, CA (*see also Rickards Ltd v Oppenheim*)	64
Charnock v Liverpool Corp [1968] 1 WLR 1498, CA	64
Cine Bes Filmcilik Ve Yapim Click v UIP [2003] EWCA Civ 1699	124
City Inn Ltd v Shepherd Construction Ltd [2003] 1 BLR 468	76
Clark Contracts v The Burrell Co [2002] SLT 103	30
Clydebank Engineering and Shipbuilding Company Ltd v Don Jose Ramos Yzquierdo y Castenada [1905] AC 6, HL	116, 126, 139
Construction Award No 2/6 (1995) 2 Con LYB 57	11
Construction Award No 3 (1994) Const LY 65	39
Costain Building and Civil Engineering v Scottish Rugby Union plc (1993) 69 BLR 80	36
Costain Civil Engineering Ltd and another v Zanen Dredging and Contracting Company Ltd (1996) 85 BLR 77	17, 22
Countrywide Communications Ltd v ICL Pathway Ltd (2000) CLC 324	17
Croudace Ltd v London Borough of Lambeth (1986) 33 BLR 20	36, 39
Cutter v Powell (1795) 6 TR 320	1
Dalkia Utilities Services Plc v Celtech International Ltd [2006] EWHC 63	198
Dallman v King (1837) 7 LJCP 6	34
Dodd v Churton [1897] 1 QB 562	68
Dunlop Pneumatic Tyre Company v New Garage and Motor Company Ltd [1915] AC 79	124
Ellis Tylin Ltd v Co-operative Retail Services Ltd [1999] 1 BLR 205	191
ERDC Construction Ltd v HM Love & Co (1994) 70 BLR 67	15
ERDC Group Ltd v Brunel University [2006] BLR 255	24
Fairweather (H) v Wandsworth LBC (1987) 39 BLR 106	153
Feather (Thomas) v Keighley Corporation (1953) 52 LCR 30	199
Felton v Wharrie (1906) 2 Hudson's BC (4th edn) 398	106
FG Minter Ltd v WHTSO (1980) 13 BLR 1, CA	166
Franks & Collingwood v Gates (1983) 1 Con LR 21	7

Table of cases

Gaymark Investments Pty Ltd v Walter Construction Group Ltd [1999] NTSC 143; (2005) 21 Const LJ (Australia)	74
George Fisher Holding Ltd v Multi Design Consultants (1998) 61 Con LR 85	173
Gilbert & Partners v Knight [1968] 2 All ER 248	13
GLC v Cleveland Bridge & Engineering (1984) 34 BLR 50	65
Great Eastern Hotel Company Ltd v John Laing Construction [2005] EWHC 181; 99 Con LR 45, TCC	182, 185
Hadley Design Associates Ltd v The Lord Mayor and Citizens of the City of Westminster [2003] EWHC 1617, TCC; (2004) TCLR 1	192
Henry Boot Construction Ltd v Alstom Combined Cycles Ltd [2005] BLR 437	36, 148
Henry Boot Construction (UK) Ltd v Malmaison Hotel (Manchester) Ltd [1999] All ER 118; 70 Con LR 32	111
Hersent Offshore SA and Amsterdamse Ballast Betonen Waterbouw BV v Burmah Oil Tankers Ltd (1978) 10 BLR 1	53
Hick v Raymond & Reid [1893] AC 22	63
Hickman v Roberts [1913] AC 229	38
Hoenig v Isaacs [1952] 2 All ER 176	2, 6, 199
Holland Hannen & Cubitts v WHTSO (1981) 18 BLR 80	3
Holme v Guppy (1838) 3 M&W 387	67
Hutchinson v Harris (1978) 10 BLR 19	5
ICI v Bovis Construction Ltd (1993) Con LR 90	179
IJS Contractors Ltd v Dew Construction Ltd (2000) 85 Con LR 48	201
James Longley & Co Ltd v South West Thames Regional Health Authority (1983) 25 BLR 56	174
J Crosby & Son v Portland UTC (1967) 5 BLR 121	180
Jeancharm Limited (t/a Beaver International) v Barnet Football Club Limited [2003] EWCA Civ 58	127
Jennings Construction v Birt QM Ltd [1987] 8 NSWLR 18	54
J F Finnegan Ltd v Community HA Ltd (1995) 77 BLR 22	137
J F Finnegan Ltd v Sheffield City Council (1988) 43 BLR 124	159

Table of cases

Case	Page
J M Hill & Sons v London Borough of Camden (1980) 18 BLR 31	107, 194, 200
John Barker Construction Ltd v London Portman Hotel Ltd (1996) 83 BLR 31; (1996) 12 Const LJ 277	73, 167, 185
John F Hunt v ASME Engineering Ltd [2007] CILL 2496	171
John Holland Construction and Engineering Pty Ltd v Kvaerner RJ Brown Pty Ltd (1996) 82 BLR 83	180
John Holland Property Ltd v Hunter Valley Earth Moving [2003] Const LJ 171	179
John Jarvis v Rockdale Housing Association (1986) 36 BLR 48	195
John Mowlem & Co plc v Eagle Star Insurance Co Ltd & Others (1993) 62 BLR 126	42
Jones and another v St John's College Oxford (1870) LR 6 QB 115	123
Kelly Pipelines Ltd v British Gas plc (1989) 48 BLR 126	10
Kemp v Rose (1858) 1 Giff 258	133
KNS Industrial Services (Birmingham) Ltd v Sindall Ltd (2000) 75 Con LR 1	28
Laing & Morrison-Knudsen v Aegon Insurance Co (1997) 86 BLR 70	197
Laing Management (Scotland) Ltd v John Doyle Construction Ltd (Scotland) [2004] BLR 295	181
Lancaster v John Kim Bird (1999) 73 Con LR 22	8
Laserbore Ltd v Morrison Biggs Wall Ltd [1993] CILL 896	21
Leedsford v City of Bradford (1956) 24 BLR 45	46
Lockland Builders Ltd v Rickwood (1995) 77 BLR 38	197
Lombard South Central Plc v Butterworth [1987] QB 527, CA	108
London Borough of Hounslow v Twickenham Garden Developments (1970) 7 BLR 89; (1971) Ch 333	188
London Borough of Merton v Stanley Hugh Leach Ltd (1985) 32 BLR 51	69, 153, 180
London Scottish Benefit Society v Chorley (1884) 13 QBD 872	174

Table of cases

Case	Page
London Underground Limited v Citylink Telecommunications Limited [2007] EWHC 1749, TCC	182
Lubenham Fidelities & Investments Company Ltd v South Pembrokeshire District Council (1986) 33 BLR 39	35, 194
Lucas v Godwin (1837) 3 Bing NC 737	106
Lusty v Finsbury Securities Ltd (1991) 58 BLR 66	21
McAlpine Humberoak v McDermott International (1992) 58 BLR 1, CA	110, 122, 180
McAlpine v Tilebox [2005] BLR 271; [2005] EWHC 281 (TCC)	77, 118, 129
Malkinson v Trimm [2002] EWCA Civ 1273	174
Manakee v Brattle [1970] 1 WLR 1607	173
Melville Dundas Ltd (in receivership) v George Wimpey UK Ltd [2007] 1 WLR 1136	31
M J Gleeson plc v Taylor Woodrow Construction Ltd (1989) 49 BLR 95	120
Mid-Glamorgan County Council v J Devonald Williams & Partner (1992) 29 Con LR 129	180
Millers Specialist Joinery v Nobles Construction, 3 August 2000, unreported, HHJ Gilliland QC	29
Minster Trust v Traps Tractors Ltd [1954] 1 WLR 963	35
Mitsui Construction v Attorney General of Hong Kong (1986) 33 BLR 1	9
Mowlem Plc (t/a Mowlem Marine) v Stena Line Ports Ltd [2004] EWHC 2206, TCC	19
Mowlem Plc v PHI Group Ltd [2004] BLR 421	20
Multiplex Constructions (UK) Ltd v Honeywell Control Systems Ltd (No 2) [2007] EWHC 447, TCC	78
Murray v Leisureplay [2005] EWCA Civ 963	118, 128
Neodox v Swinton and Pendlebury BC (1958) 5 BLR 38	46
Northern Developments (Cumbria) Ltd v J&J Nichol [2000] BLR 158	28
Oxford University Press v John Stedman Group (1990) 34 Con LR 1	169
Panamena Europea Navigacion v Leyland [1947] AC 428	38
Parkinson v Commissioners of Works [1949] 2 KB 632	12

Case	Page
Patman and Fotheringham v Pilditch (1904) Hudson's BC (4th edn) vol. 2, p. 368	48
Pavey and Matthews Proprietary Ltd v Paul (1987) 6 Const LJ 59	15, 21
Peak Construction Ltd v McKinney Foundations Ltd (1970) 1 BLR 111	70, 107, 117, 121, 160
Peninsula Balmain Pty Ltd v Abigroup Contractors Pty Ltd [2002] NSWCA 211 (Australia)	76
Perini Corporation v Commonwealth of Australia (1969) 12 BLR 82	39
Phee Farrar Jones Ltd v Connaught Mason Ltd [2003] CILL 2005	163
Phillips Hong Kong Ltd v The Attorney General of Hong Kong (1993) 61 BLR 41	126
Pierce Design v International Ltd v Mark Johnston & another [2007] EWHC 1691, TCC	32
Pigott Foundations v Shepherd Construction (1993) 67 BLR 48	120
Rapid Building v Ealing Family Housing (1984) 29 BLR 5	123, 131
Re Nossen's Letter Patent [1969] 1 WLR 638	175
Re Yeadon Waterworks Co v Wright (1895) 72 LT 832, CA	139
Rees & Kirby Ltd v Swansea City Council (1985) 30 BLR 1, CA	154, 166
Regalian Properties v London Docklands Development Corporation [1995] 1 WLR 212	16
Reinwood Ltd v L Brown & Sons [2007] 1 BLR 10	195
Rice v Great Yarmouth Borough Council [2000] TLR 26 July	201
Richards & Wallington (Plant Hire) Ltd v A Monk & Co Ltd, 11 June 1984, unreported	176
Rickards Ltd v Oppenheim [1950] 1 KB 616, CA (*see also Charles Rickards*)	107
Riverside Property Investments v Blackhawk Automotive [2004] All ER (D) 264	163
Robin Ellis Ltd v Vinexsa International Ltd [2003] BLR 373	192
Royal Brompton Hospital NHS Trust v Hammond and Others (No. 7) (2001) 76 Con LR 148; [2002] EWHC 2037, TCC	112, 114, 185

Table of cases

Case	Page
Rupert Morgan Building Services (LLC) Ltd v Jervis (David) and Jervis (Harriet) [2004] BLR 18	31
R W Green Ltd v Cade Bros Farms [1978] 1 Lloyd's Rep 602	118
Sanjay Lachhani v Destination Canada (UK) Ltd (1997) 13 Const LJ 279	23
Scheldebouw BV v St James Homes (Grosvenor Dock) Ltd [2006] BLR 124	41
Serck Controls Ltd v Drake & Scull Engineering Ltd (1997) 13 Const LJ 279	24
Sharpe v San Paulo Railways (1873) LR 8 Ch App 597	45, 48
Shawton Engineering Ltd v DGP Ltd [2006] BLR 1, CA	65, 109, 202
Sheffield v Conrad (1987) 22 Con LR 108	200
Shore v Horwitz Construction Co Ltd v Franki of Canada Ltd [1964] SCR 589, Canada SC	157
Sindall Ltd v Solland (2001) 80 Con LR 152	75
Sisu Capital Fund Ltd v Tucker & others [2006] 1 All ER 167	177
Skanska Construction UK Ltd v Egger (Baronry) Ltd [2004] EWHC 1748, TCC	185
S L Timber Systems Ltd v Carillion [2001] BLR 516	29
SMK Cabinets v Hili Modern Electrics Pty [1984] VR 391 (Australia)	121
Societa Finanziara Industrie Turistiche SpA v di Balsorano, 30 June 2006, unreported	178
Stanor Electric v R Mansell [1988] CILL 399	135
Stephen Donald Architects Ltd v King (2003) 94 Con LR 1	19
Stockport MBC v O'Reilly [1978] 1 Lloyd's Rep 595	49
Strachan & Henshaw Ltd v Stein Industrie (UK) Ltd and GEC Alsthom Ltd (1997) EWCA Civ 2940	150
Sunley (B) & Co Ltd v Cunard White Star Ltd [1940] 1 KB 740, CA	158, 166
Surrey Heath Borough Council v Lovell Construction Ltd (1988) 15 Con LR 68	119
Sutcliffe v Chippendale and Edmondson (1971) 18 BLR 157	199
Tara Civil Engineering Ltd v Moorfield Developments Ltd (1989) 46 BLR 72	190
Tate & Lyle Distribution v GLC [1982] 1 WLR 149	161, 165
Taylor v Bhail (1995) Con LR 70	16

Temloc Ltd v Errill Properties (1987) 39 BLR 30	133
Tergeste, The (1903) P 26	7
Tern Construction Group v RBS Garages Ltd (1992) 34 Con LR 137	4
Tersons Ltd v Stevenage Development Corporation [1965] 1 QB 37; (1977) 5 BLR 54	53, 117
Tharsis Sulphur & Copper Company v McElroy & Sons (1878) 3 App Cas 1040	50
Thorn v London Corp (1876) 1 App Cas 120	49
Tony Cox (Dismantlers) v Jim 5 Ltd (1997) 13 Const LJ 209	8
Trimis v Mina (2000) 2 TCLR 346	17
Trolloppe & Colls Ltd v North West Metropolitan Regional Hospital Board [1973] 1 WLR 601	71
Trustees of Stratfield Saye Estate v AHL Construction Ltd [2004] EWHC 3286, TCC	52
Try Build Ltd v Invicta Tennis Ltd (2000) 71 Con LR 140	162
Turner Corporation Ltd (Receiver and Manager Appointed) v Austotel Pty Ltd (1997) 13 BCL 378	74
Turner Page Music v Torres Design Associates [1997] CILL 1263	5
Walter Lawrence and Son Ltd v Commercial Union Properties (1984) 4 Con LR 37	72
Watts, Watts & Co v Mitsui [1917] AC 227, HL	131
Wharf Properties v Eric Cumine Associates (No. 2) (1991) 52 BLR 1	179
Whittaker v Dunn (1887) 3 TLR 602	9
Whittall Builders Co Ltd v Chester-le-Street DC (1985) 12 Con LJ 356	157, 158, 165
William Lacey (Houslow) Ltd v Davis [1957] 1 WLR 932	13
Williams v Fitzmaurice (1858) 3 H & N 844	45
Wiltshier Construction (South) Ltd v Parkers Developments Ltd (1997) 13 Const LJ 129	190
Wormald Engineering Ltd v Resources Conservation International (1988) 8 BCL 158	54

Introduction

The construction of a building will often take longer than expected, and cost more than expected. The work may be technically challenging from a design or a construction perspective. The relationships between developers, contractors, subcontractors and professionals usually give rise to legal complications. The contract may be too simple or too complicated. In short, even the simplest of projects have the potential to give rise to a myriad of disagreements.

This book focuses on construction claims. We have attempted to focus more on contractor claims, although the chapters dealing with liquidated damages and termination both relate to claims brought by employers. (The other principal complaint by employers, namely the existence of defects, is dealt with in a separate title in this series, *Building Defects*.)

Contractors' claims, inevitably, often arise out of non-payment. A contractor's claim might typically comprise three parts: payment of the original contract sum, payment for additional works, or variations, and payment for other losses caused by reason of delay to the project or disruption. Chapter 1 therefore focuses upon payment claims, and considers the different sorts of contract that exist (lump sum, remeasurement, etc.). Chapter 1 also includes how payment claims are affected by the *Housing Grants, Construction and Regeneration Act* 1996.

Most building contracts are governed by some sort of certification process, in order to progress payment during the course of the work and final payment. Certification is a sufficiently important topic in relation to construction claims to be considered separately, in Chapter 2.

What is additional work? On what basis should additional work be valued? Of what effect are notification provisions in relation to variations? These and other questions are addressed in cases summarised in Chapter 3.

Introduction

Chapters 4, 5 and 6 consider questions of delay and disruption. From a contractor's point of view, these issues relate to the obtaining of extensions of time, and claiming loss and expense. From an employer's perspective, this usually means levying liquidated damages. These complicated issues give rise to numerous difficult questions, which are tackled by site teams, construction professionals, adjudicators, arbitrators and judges on a daily basis. Case law sheds considerable light on the proper approaches to be adopted by those advancing and those defending these claims.

Finally, Chapter 7 deals with termination and repudiatory breach. Construction claims will often include consideration of whether a contract has been terminated lawfully and, if not, what the consequences may be. The cases selected for summary are intended to illustrate the practical application of generally accepted legal principles.

1
Payment claims

The basis upon which a contractor is entitled to payment depends upon the type of contract. Whilst the *Housing Grants, Construction and Regeneration Act* 1996 imposes certain rights where the contract is silent, it is up to the parties to decide when and how payment is to be made.

1.1 LUMP SUM CONTRACT

The most basic type of contract is an entire contract, which is a form of lump sum contract where entire performance is required prior to payment being made. Most lump sum contracts nowadays, however, have arrangements by which the contractor is paid in instalments, dependent upon either progress made or time, or in some more complex contracts, a combination of the two.

Substantial performance is the principle whereby defects or omissions in an otherwise complete building cannot be used as the basis of depriving the contractor of payment. The employer has to pay the contract price, against which is deducted (or 'abated') the cost of carrying out the omitted work or rectifying the defective work. (See *Case in Point: Building Defects* for cases which deal with the basis upon which, for example, the cost of defective work is assessed.)

Cutter v Powell (1795)

An entire contract is an indivisible contract, where the entire fulfilment of the promise by either party is a condition precedent to the right to call for the fulfilment of any part of the promise by the other.

Appleby v Myers (1867)

The claimants contracted to erect machinery on the defendant's premises at specific prices for particular portions, and to keep it in repair for two years. The price was to be paid upon completion of all of the work. After some of the work had been carried out, when other works were still in the course of completion, the premises and all of the machinery and materials were destroyed in a fire. It was held that both parties were to be excused from future performance of the contract, but the claimants were not entitled to claim in respect of those parts of the work which had been completed, whether or not the materials used had become the property of the defendant.

Hoenig v Isaacs (1952)

The claimant was contracted by the defendant to decorate and furnish the latter's flat for £750. The contract stated: 'net cash, as the work proceeds, and balance on completion'. The defendant, by instalments, paid £400 of the agreed price and kept the furniture, but, when sued for the balance, refused to pay any more and argued that he was not liable to pay anything under the contract at all because of certain defects in the furniture. The ground on which he based this claim was that the contract was an entire contract, that the plaintiff could not sue for any part of the purchase price unless and until he had wholly performed his obligations thereunder, and that this was a condition precedent which had never been fulfilled. This was rejected.

When a contract provides for a specific sum to be paid on completion of specified work, the courts lean against a construction of the contract which would deprive the contractor of any payment at all simply because there are some defects or omissions.

Each case turns on the construction of the contract.

Bolton v Mahadeva (1972)

The claimant was contracted to install a boiler system in the defendant's home at a cost of £560. The claimant brought a claim for the sum plus an additional amount for extras. The defendant asserted numerous defects in the work, and that the claimant had failed to perform the contract. It was alleged that the consideration for the contract had wholly failed. The claim succeeded at first instance, less the sum of £174 which was the cost to remedy the system. The Court of Appeal, however, held that in considering whether there was substantial performance, it is relevant to take into account both the nature of the defects and the proportion between the cost of rectifying them and the contract price. The appeal was allowed:

> 'The contract was a contract to install a central heating system. If a central heating system when installed is such that it does not heat the house adequately and is such, further, that fumes are given out, so as to make living rooms uncomfortable, and if the putting right of those defects is not something which can be done by some slight amendment of the system, then I think that the contract is not substantially performed.'

Holland Hannen & Cubitts v WHTSO (1981)

In a useful judgment, HHJ Newey QC summarised the state of the law:

> '(1) An entire contract is one in which what is described as "complete performance" by one party is a condition precedent to the liability of the other party.
>
> (2) Whether a contract is an entire one is a matter of construction; it depends upon what the parties agreed. A lump sum contract is not necessarily an entire contract. A contract providing for interim payments, for example, as work proceeds, but for retention money to be held until completion is usually entire as to the retention moneys, but not necessarily the interim payments.
>
> (3) The test of complete performance for the purposes of an entire contract is in fact "substantial performance".
>
> (4) What is substantial is not to be determined on a comparison of cost of work done and work omitted or done badly.
>
> (5) If a party abandons performance of the contract, he cannot recover payment for work which he has completed.

3

(6) If a party has done something different from that which he contracted to perform, then, however valuable his work, he cannot claim to have performed substantially.

(7) If a party is prevented from performing his contract by default of the other party, he is excused from performance and may recover damages.

(8) Parties may agree that, in return for one party performing certain obligations, the other will pay to him a *quantum meruit*.

(9) A contract for payment of a *quantum meruit* may be made in the same way as any other type of contract, including conduct.

(10) A contract for a *quantum meruit* will not readily be inferred from the actions of a landowner in using something which has become physically attached to his land.

(11) There may be circumstances in which, even though a special contract has not been performed there may arise a new or substituted contract; it is a matter of evidence.'

Tern Construction Group v RBS Garages Ltd (1992)

The claimant contractors agreed with the defendant to erect a car showroom and ancillary buildings, on the *JCT Standard Form of Building Contract (1980 edition)*. A preliminary issue arose as to whether substantial completion of the works (or of the works for which interim certificates had been issued) was a condition precedent to be paid in respect of those works. HHJ Newey QC held that the *JCT Standard Form*, with its elaborate and detailed provisions, dealing with many matters, but most importantly employers going into partial possession, determination of the contractors' employment without determination of the contract, and payment by instalments, was not simply a contract for the contractors to perform all or nearly all their obligations before the employers performed any of theirs. The standard term could not usefully be described as 'entire'.

The principle of substantial performance can be applied to an architect's right to payment under the stages of the *RIBA Conditions of Engagement*.

Hutchinson v Harris (1978)

The claimant engaged the defendant on the terms of the *RIBA Conditions of Engagement*, for the purposes of converting her house into flats. The defendant prepared drawings and obtained the planning permission. The claimant then entered into a building contract. When the building work had been nearly completed, the defendant made a final inspection and issued a final certificate.

The claimant then moved to another house. The defendant submitted a fee account for £800, representing the balance of the fee of 12 per cent. The claimant, however, refused to pay the defendant's account, and commenced proceedings against her claiming damages for professional negligence. The defendant counterclaimed for her fees. The judge found that the defendant was negligent in failing to obtain competitive tenders (albeit with nominal damages) and in certifying defective work, valuing the damages as the cost of remedial work. He allowed the counterclaim for the balance of the fees. The claimant appealed to the Court of Appeal on the basis that the defendant's fee should be abated by reason of her negligence. The appeal was dismissed on the basis that the defendant was entitled to the whole of her fee. To have abated or reduced it on the grounds of her negligence would have been to pay the claimant twice over – a reduction in the fee and also damages for negligence.

Turner Page Music v Torres Design Associates (1997)

The claimant employer engaged the defendant designer to provide professional services in connection with the redevelopment of a cinema. The contract price agreed with the contractor was £450,000, but the outturn cost of the project was over £800,000. The claimant sued the defendant for various breaches of duty arising out of design, costing, letting, supervising and certifying the works. The claimant claimed, amongst other things, for the full repayment of fees paid. This was described as 'hopeless': there was no total failure of consideration. The defendant plainly did a great deal of work. Insofar as they were in breach, the breaches would be recompensed accordingly, but deprivation of fees in addition would be double recovery. However, distinguishing

Hutchinson v Harris, there was no entire agreement so that the fee claim could be abated to take account of work not done.

Retention money may be held until completion if the contract so provides. Entire, as opposed to substantial, performance is required for the contractor to be entitled to payment of the retention.

Hoenig v Isaacs (1952)

Per Lord Denning:

> 'A familiar instance is when the contract provides for progress payments to be made as the work proceeds, but for retention money to be held until completion. Then entire performance is usually a condition precedent to payment of the retention money, but not, of course, to the progress payments. The contractor is entitled to payment pro rata as the work proceeds, less a deduction for retention money. But he is not entitled to the retention money until the work is entirely finished, without defects or omissions.'

However, in this case the amount withheld represented over 45 per cent of the contract price, and therefore could not be considered as a retention.

In many construction contracts, however, there will arise either by statute or by implication a right to payment in instalments, rather than payment of the entirety of the contract sum at the conclusion of the works.

However, each 'instalment' may then be treated as a mini-entire contract, requiring completion or substantial completion of the work (or period) relevant to the instalment to give rise to an entitlement to payment.

The Housing Grants, Construction and Regeneration Act 1996

Providing the contract is a 'construction contract' for the purposes of the Act, s. 109 provides a statutory entitlement to payment in instalments:

109 Entitlement to stage payments

(1) A party to a construction contract is entitled to payment by instalments, stage payments or other periodic payments for any work under the contract unless—

(a) it is specified in the contract that the duration of the work is to be less than 45 days, or

(b) it is agreed between the parties that the duration of the work is estimated to be less than 45 days.

(2) The parties are free to agree the amounts of the payments and the intervals at which, or circumstances in which, they become due.

(3) In the absence of such agreement, the relevant provisions of the Scheme for Construction Contracts apply....

The parties are free to agree the amount and timing of payment. This means that the parties could expressly agree to one payment at the end of the work. In the absence of such an agreement, however, the statute will apply. (See section 1.5 for claims under the *Housing Grants, Construction and Regeneration Act* 1996.)

The Tergeste (1903)

For the position at common law, see the judgment of Phillimore J:

'A man who contracts to do a long costly piece of work does not contract, unless he expressly says so that he will do all the work, standing out of pocket until he is paid at the end. He is entitled to say, "...there is an understanding all along that you are to give me from time to time, at the reasonable times, payments for work done."'

Whether a sum for payment under a contract might ordinarily be said to be inclusive or exclusive of value added tax turns upon the terms of the particular contract.

Franks & Collingwood v Gates (1983)

The defendant was a private individual who engaged the claimant to carry out certain construction works to his holiday home. The quotation was provided for a fixed price of £7,000. It did not bear a VAT registration number. The claimant sued the defendant for the price of the works including VAT. It was held that in such a relationship the price would be taken (unless otherwise stated) to be inclusive of VAT.

Tony Cox (Dismantlers) v Jim 5 Ltd (1997)

The claimant was a demolition specialist that had agreed to transfer land to the defendant builders and to carry out infrastructure works, for which they were to be paid £800,000 apportioned between different phases of the work. The agreement was silent as to VAT. However, VAT was payable by the defendant because it was held that there was a custom and practice within the building industry ('notorious, certain and reasonable'), in which both parties to the contract operated, that prices are quoted ex-VAT. *Franks & Collingwood v Gates* (above) was distinguished as it did not relate to a custom between those in the construction industry, but between a builder and a private individual.

Lancaster v Bird [1999]

A contract for the supply and erection of a small agricultural shed was between a builder seeking to be paid in cash and a part-time farmer. There was no evidence that it was an implied custom that VAT would be paid on top of the cash payments. The 'officious bystander', when asked whether the parties to a such a transaction intended that VAT should be paid on top of the cash payments, would say: 'No, of course that was not the intention of the parties.'

Chadwick LJ said that, whilst it would normally be made expressly clear, the question whether the price for a building contract was inclusive or exclusive of VAT turned on the terms of the particular contract. It was in the interests of the builder to make it clear because, as between the builder and the Commissioners for Customs and Excise, the builder would be liable to pay VAT on the goods and services provided. If the builder failed to make it plain to the employer that he was stipulating payment of VAT in addition to the contract price, he would be left to account to the Revenue for the VAT out of what he receives.

1.2 REMEASUREMENT CONTRACT

A remeasurement contract is where the work is measured and valued against agreed rates. There is therefore no agreement as to a lump sum, but there is agreement as to the basis upon which the work will be valued. Often, the nature of the work will be known, but the extent will not (for example, in running pipework or electrical cabling).

The same issues may arise in a remeasurement contract in relation to payment upon substantial completion. There is nothing peculiar to a remeasurement contract that prevents it from being an entire contract.

Whittaker v Dunn (1887)

The contract was to construct a floor to a laundry to consist of a kind of granite concrete of a certain thickness, so as to form a hard and homogeneous flooring to three rooms, to be paid at so much per square yard and paid upon completion. The project manager, to whose satisfaction the work was required to be, stated that in relation to two rooms the work was not to specification. The contractor sued for the price of the work. The Court considered that as the work had not been carried out, the contractors were not entitled to payment.

It may be possible, depending upon the wording of the contract, to vary agreed rates where the quantities in fact change sufficiently so as to change the nature of the work undertaken.

Mitsui v Attorney General of Hong Kong (1986)

The claimant contractors agreed with the defendant Government to excavate and construct a tunnel from Ma Mei Ha to Nam Chung. It was accepted that the nature of the ground through which the tunnel was to pass could not be predicted accurately in advance. The contract therefore specified different linings, suitable for different ground conditions, but did not specify where lining was to be required or of what type, which would be decided by the engineer as the work proceeded. The bills of quantities was priced by the contractors with reference to estimated lengths of tunnel which either were to be left unlined, or were to be lined with each of the different types of lining respectively.

Clause 74(4) of the contract provided:

> 'If the nature or amount of any omission or addition relative to the nature or amount of the Works or to any part thereof shall be such that in the opinion of the Engineer the rate contained in the Contract for any item of the Works is by reason of such omission or addition rendered unreasonable or inapplicable then a suitable rate shall be agreed upon between the Engineer and the Contractor'

The estimates in the bills were wildly wrong and the extent of linings (and the most expensive lining) required increased substantially. The Privy Council considered whether the additional quantities gave rise to additional payment under clause 74(4). Lord Bridge, finding for the contractors, stated:

> '... If the contract documents were understood in the sense contended for by the Government, engineering contractors tendering for the work would have two options. They could either gamble on encountering more or less favourable ground conditions or they could anticipate the worst case and price their tenders accordingly....It follows that, if the Government are right, there is a large element of wagering inherent in this contract. It seems to their Lordships somewhat improbable that a responsible public authority on the one hand and responsible engineering contractors on the other, contracting for the execution of public works worth many millions of dollars, should deliberately embark on a substantial gamble.... By contrast, if the Contractors' submission is correct, ...the rates can be suitably adjusted. Given the inherent uncertainty as to the scope of the work that will be required, a provision to this effect would seem an eminently sensible means of ensuring that the Contractors receive no less, and the Government pay no more, than a reasonable price for the work actually done.'

Kelly Pipelines Ltd v British Gas plc (1989)

The defendants employed the claimants to lay mains and provide maintenance services. The contract covered a period of two years and provided that the claimants would have available for use on the contract a maximum of 46 and a minimum of 30 non-supervisory teams. Over the two-year period of the contract, the defendant employed an average of only 28 gangs per week. The claimant sued for £78,000 in respect of the loss of indirect site costs, overheads and profit as a result of the defendant's failure to employ 30 gangs per week. The relevant clause of the contract provided that if, in relation to any part of the works executed, there was no appropriate rate or price in the contract, or the contract rate was unreasonable or inapplicable, then the engineer should determine a reasonable and proper rate or price. However, the Court held that the engineer was not entitled to take into account the decrease in the number of gangs, in assessing whether the contract rate was reasonable or unreasonable.

Construction Award No 2/6 (1995)

The claimant contractors agreed to lay pipeline beneath a road for the local authority employer. The bill of quantities underestimated the quantity of deep tarmac, allowing a very high rate. The engineer sought to re-rate this item under clause 56(2) of the *ICE Conditions of Contract (5th edition)*. The arbitrator noted the consensus amongst commentators that the decision under this clause must exclude circumstances where the contractor might, as a result of an error gamble, make a substantial loss or gain as a result of an increase or decrease in the quantity of an item. However, it was held that the circumstances warranted a review of the rate. This was because the bill item was expressed as a 'small quantity' item, with sufficient clarity to enable an experienced contractor to recognise it as such; the conditions in fact encountered were continuous, or virtually so, for the whole length of the pipeline, requiring, or enabling, the contractor to employ techniques different from those which would have been required for the billed item and it was therefore the increase in quantity, of itself, that changed the nature of the work and the conditions under which it was executed. In setting a new rate, the arbitrator related it as far as was practicable to the relevant bill rate.

1.3 PRIME COST CONTRACT

The basis of payment in a prime cost or cost plus contract is the actual cost of completing the work, together with an additional element for overheads and/or profit. There are varying levels of complexity in determining actual costs and for the determining the uplift which, in modern contracts, might often include 'pain' or 'gain', dependent upon achieving a target outturn cost.

1.4 QUANTUM MERUIT

This phrase is used to refer to a reasonable sum. It generally becomes relevant as the basis of a payment claim where:

- There is an express agreement to pay a reasonable sum.
- There is no agreement as to what the payment should be.
- There is no contract at all, or there is a 'quasi-contract'. This may be the result of work having been carried out in the expectation of entering into a contract. however, in not all cases of failed negotiations, where work has been carried out, does the obligation to pay a reasonable sum arise.
- Work is undertaken outside the scope of the contract.
- Work is undertaken under an unenforceable or void contract (but not an illegal contract).

Parkinson v Commissioners of Works (1949)

The claimant contractors agreed with the defendant to erect an ordnance factory according to various specifications for the contract sum of £3,500,000. Under a contract term, the defendant had power, at their absolute discretion, to modify the extent and character of the work or to order alterations of or additions to the works. By a variation, the method of payment was to be ascertained on the basis of such net rates or prices as should be agreed upon between the architect and contractors, or failing agreement, should be fixed by arbitration. It was further agreed that the sum eventually to be paid to the contractors should not be less than actual cost to them, as defined, plus a net profit or remuneration of £150,000, and not more than actual cost plus a net profit of £300,000.

The defendant ordered work to be executed greatly in excess of the amount contemplated, although not different in character. The actual cost to the contractors was £6,683,056, which amount had been paid to the contractor along with the £300,000 maximum profit. The contractors claimed a net profit in excess of the £300,000 fixed by the contract. The Court held that the work which was contemplated at the time at which the deed of variation was executed was that which was to be executed under the original contract plus perhaps a further £500,000 worth of work. Under the contract as varied the contractors would not have been bound to continue making alterations and additions, if ordered, for years and years, without any extra payment by way of profit. That would have led to manifest absurdity and injustice. The claimant executed the additional work at the request of the defendant, and they were entitled to be paid a reasonable profit or remuneration in respect of it.

William Lacey (Houslow) Ltd v Davis (1957)

The claimant was invited by the defendant to tender for renovations and construction work on a war-torn building. Having done so, the claimant was informed that his tender had been the lowest and he was led to believe that he would receive a contract. The claimant was then asked to provide various estimates for the purposes of obtaining the licences then necessary, and also a number of further estimates based on altered plans. The defendant subsequently decided not to proceed with the work and instead sold the house. It was held that the builder was entitled to be paid a *quantum meruit* for the work he had done, because the work extended well beyond the kind of work a builder would have been expected to do gratuitously in the hope of obtaining a contract.

Gilbert & Partners v Knight (1968)

For a fee of £30, the surveyor claimant agreed to prepare drawings, to arrange tenders, to obtain consents and to settle the accounts for certain proposed alterations to the defendant's property, and to supervise the work of alteration, the cost of which was estimated at roughly £600. When the builder had started work, the owner ordered some more work, bringing the total cost to £2,283. The claimant did not say anything more to the defendant about charges; the defendant did not say anything more to the claimant. The surveyor supervised the additional work. When the work was finished, the claimant submitted an account for £135, being the agreed £30 plus 100 guineas, a scale fee for supervising the additional work. The defendant paid only the agreed £30.

The Court of Appeal applied the dicta of Lord Dunedin in *Steven v Bromley & Son* (1919) in the context of a charterparty case:

> 'As regards *quantum meruit* where there are two parties who are under contract *quantum meruit* must be a new contract, and in order to have a new contract you must get rid of the old contract.'

The Court considered that these parties had not get rid of the old contract. The defendant was entitled to assume that it was still running between them, and that she would not be asked for a different sum on a different basis.

British Steel Corp v Cleveland Bridge & Engineering (1984)

The defendants successfully tendered for the fabrication of steel work in the construction of a building. The defendants sent a letter of intent to the claimants which (i) recorded the defendants' intention to enter into a contract with the claimant, (ii) proposed that the contract be on the defendants' standard form and (iii) requested the plaintiffs to commence work immediately 'pending the preparation and issuing to you of the official form of sub-contract'. There were further discussions as to the proper specifications, which were changed extensively. The claimants went ahead with the manufacture and delivery of the products. When all but one of the nodes had been delivered, delivery of the remaining elements was held up due to an industrial dispute. The defendants refused to make any interim or final payment and instead claimed for late delivery, or delivery of the nodes out of sequence. The claimants sued for the value of the steelwork on a *quantum meruit*, contending that no binding contract had been entered into.

It was held, on the facts, that an executory contract had not been created by the claimants beginning to manufacture following receipt of the letter of intent, because the parties were still negotiating. Given those negotiations, it was impossible to determine the extent of the liability. Because the parties had not been able to reach agreement on the price or other essential terms, the contract was not entered into. The defendants were therefore obliged to pay a reasonable sum for the work done pursuant to the claimants' request.

Pavey and Matthews Proprietary Ltd v Paul (1987)

The claimant builder claimed for the value of work done and materials supplied pursuant to an oral building contract. By virtue of the *Builders Licensing Act* 1971 (NSW), an oral contract between an employer and a builder holding a licence was not enforceable. The action upon the basis of a *quantum meruit* succeeded because it rested not on an implied term of the (unenforceable) contract, but on a claim to restitution based on unjust enrichment. However, the quasi-contractual obligation to pay a fair and just compensation for a benefit which has been accepted will only arise in a case where this is no applicable genuine agreement or where such an agreement is frustrated, avoided or unenforceable.

ERDC Construction Ltd v HM Love & Co (1994)

The defendants engaged the claimant contractors to carry out repairs to the defendants' premises under the *JCT Standard Form of Building Contract, Private with Quantities, 1963 edition (July 1977 revision)*, as amended. The claimants claimed damages for breach of contract and, in the alternative, the payment of the sum of £276,388.95 as a reasonable remuneration for the work executed.

The Court held that there was no suggestion that the claimants ever intimated that they were treating any breach of contract as fundamental and were rescinding the contract. For this reason, there was no basis for the claim made upon quantum meruit. Far from rescinding the contract, the claimants all along had claimed to have performed their duties under the contract and they had sought payment under the contract. Having elected not to rescind the contract but to proceed with the contract, they must be held to have waived any claim for anything more than the contract price.

Regalian Properties v London Docklands Development Corporation (1995)

In 1986 the claimants tendered a sum of £18.5m for a licence to build as and when the defendant owners of the land obtained vacant possession of separate parts of it. The defendant accepted the offer subject to '(1) contract (2) the district valuer's certificate of market value (3) your scheme achieving the desired design quality and the obtaining of detailed planning consent.'

By 1988 the value of residential property had fallen to an extent which made the proposed development uneconomic for the plaintiffs on the terms agreed. No contract was ever entered into. The claimants claimed from the defendant significant sums that had been incurred on fees paid to experts of one sort or another both for the purpose of producing detailed designs for the proposed development, obtaining detailed costings and in commissioning site investigations etc. in preparation for a speedy start to the development once the building lease was entered into. The claim failed. It was held that each party to the negotiations must be taken to have known (as the claimant did in the present case) that pending the conclusion of a binding contract, any cost incurred by him in preparation for the intended contract would be incurred at his own risk, in the sense that he would have no recompense for those costs if no contract resulted. By deliberate use of the words 'subject to contract' with the admitted intention that they should have their usual effect, the parties each accepted that in the event of no contract being entered into, any resultant loss should lie where it fell.

Taylor v Bhail (1995)

The building contractor claimant was engaged to carry out repairs to storm damage at a school, of which the defendant was headmaster. The work was covered by insurance. The defendant told the claimant that if he inflated the contract fee by £1,000 and gave him that sum, the claimant would get the work. The claimant sued for payment for the work done. The claim failed. If parties conspire to defraud an insurance company, they cannot expect the court to assist them in implementing their agreement.

Costain Civil Engineering Ltd and another v Zanen Dredging and Contracting Company Ltd (1996)

The appellant joint venture acted as the main contractor for the construction of the A55 Conwy Bypass and river crossing in Wales. The respondent subcontractor was responsible for various dredging operations. On appeal in relation to issues of law, the Court upheld the arbitrator's award that the respondent was entitled to a sum by way of a quantum meruit in respect of marina work that it had performed outside the subcontract. The Court held that in respect of quantum meruit, there is a distinction to be drawn between cases involving an implied term for payment, and those where there is no contract and hence the assessment is based upon restitution and unjust enrichment. This was a case that fell into the latter category.

Trimis v Mina (2000)

It was held that the fundamental starting point is that no restitutionary claims, especially claims for work done or goods supplied, can be brought while an inconsistent contractual promise subsists between the parties in relation to the subject-matter of the claim. This ensures that the law does not countenance two conflicting sets of legal obligations subsisting concurrently. If there is a valid and enforceable agreement governing the claimant's right to payment, there is 'neither occasion nor legal justification for the law to superimpose or impute an obligation or promise to pay a reasonable remuneration.'

Countrywide Communications Ltd v ICL Pathway Ltd (2000)

A consortium was assembled to make a bid for a substantial contract. Preparation for making the bid involved the members of the consortium in considerable amounts of work. The expectation was that, if the bid succeeded, the members of the consortium would be rewarded through payments made under the resulting contract. If no contract was obtained it was recognised that there would be no recompense for work done. The bid was successful, but one of the members of the consortium was then excluded from participation in the resultant contract. The Court held a right to payment on a *quantum meruit* basis. It considered that appropriate factors would be:

- whether the services were of a kind which would normally be given free of charge;
- the terms in which the request to perform the services was made (e.g. whether expressed to be 'subject to contract');
- the nature of the benefit which has resulted to the defendants — whether it was 'real' (although the performance of the services might of itself be sufficient to constitute a benefit);
- the circumstances in which the anticipated contract might not materialise and whether in particular they might be said to involve 'fault' on the part of the defendant, or to be outside the scope of the risk undertaken by the claimant at the outset.

A L Barnes Ltd v Time Talk (UK) Ltd (2003)

The claimant contractor was engaged by the defendant employer as a shop fitting contractor. There was no agreement as to price. There was simply an agreement that work would be done at particular sites. The claimant claimed a reasonable remuneration for work done.

It had been discovered that the claimant was charging for the project manager, although he was engaged and also being paid by the defendant. The judge concluded that the claimant's director had dishonestly assisted in a breach of trust to the defendant. The defendant submitted that, as a consequence of this dishonesty, the claimant could not recover any part of their claim. It was submitted that the claim must fail, because the arrangement for the project manager to be doubly paid was an integral part of the contractual relationship between the parties and the whole claim must fail because it was tainted with that illegality. However, the Court of Appeal held that the private arrangement between the project manager and director of the defendant, to which the claimant's director dishonestly lent his assistance, was not an integral (or, indeed, any) part of the contract made between their principals. That contract was for reasonable remuneration for work done. The Court of Appeal held that in the absence of agreement it is for the court to assess the remuneration, as the judge did.

Stephen Donald Architects Ltd v King (2003)

The claimant architect was a friend of the defendant, who intended to redevelop a property to provide a business premises. There were numerous discussions about the possible redevelopment, a number of which took place in public houses, during which 'the enthusiasm of the participants in the conversation for pressing ahead with the scheme was reinforced by liquid refreshment.' Nothing was agreed definitely, but the contemplation was that the likely means by which the claimant would be compensated for his contribution to the development was by the grant to him of a lease of one of the flats. The claimant undertook architectural work, including obtaining planning permission. However, it was held that the claimant had undertaken the risk in relation to his work up to the point at which a building contract might have been concluded, either that sufficient finance would not be arranged or that the terms of the finance might be perceived by the defendant as unsatisfactory. Since the project did not come to fruition, the claim for payment on a *quantum meruit* basis failed.

Mowlem Plc (t/a Mowlem Marine) v Stena Line Ports Ltd (2004)

It was common ground that the works were undertaken by Mowlem pursuant to a series of letters of intent written on behalf of Stena. It was also common ground that each of the relevant letters of intent took effect in law as an offer capable of acceptance so as to bring into existence what was described in British Steel *(above)* as *'an "if" contract'*, that is to say a contract under which A requests B to carry out a certain performance and promises B that, if he does so, he will receive a certain performance in return, usually remuneration. The last letter of intent included a promise to pay 'such reasonable amounts as can be substantiated in respect of your costs for orders placed or work done', up to a maximum of £10m. Mowlem in fact carried out work it alleged exceeded this maximum value.

It was argued that it was an implied term of the contract created by Mowlem's acceptance of the last letter that if Stena permitted Mowlem to carry out the works beyond that date and/or so that they exceeded that value, then Stena would pay a reasonable sum for those works. The Court rejected this argument on the basis that there was no justification in law for any such implication. It was found that Stena had not conducted itself in such a way as to lead Mowlem to believe that it would not seek to rely upon the terms of the letter dated 4 July 2003. The New South Wales Court of Appeal judgment in *Trimis v Mina* (above) was applied as a correct statement of the law in England and Wales.

Mowlem PLC v PHI Group Ltd (2004)

The claimant subcontracted earthworks and the associated design and construction of retaining walls to the defendant. One issue between the parties was the claimant's claim for the cost of the supply to the defendant of a crusher and of attendant plant for use by the defendant.

The arbitrator rejected this claim on the basis of lack of legal entitlement, finding that there was no express agreement by the defendant to pay for the crusher and that none was to be implied. The arbitrator also rejected a claim for payment based on a *quantum meruit* because there had been a considerable benefit to the claimant in putting lumps of concrete through the crusher, thereby rendering it suitable for use as fill, when otherwise the claimant would have had to pay for it to be carted away off site. The Court confirmed, on appeal, that the correct legal position was that it was for the claimant to establish that in all the circumstances it was entitled to be paid for the crusher. The finding was that the supply was, as a matter of fact, for the mutual benefit of the parties and thus there had been no error in law in rejecting the *quantum meruit* claim.

If there is an obligation to pay a reasonable sum, what is the basis of assessment?

Pavey and Matthews Proprietary Ltd v Paul (1987)

For the facts, see above. The Court held that, ordinarily, fair and just compensation for the benefit or enrichment accepted will correspond to the fair value of the benefit provided (e.g. remuneration at a reasonable rate for work actually done, or the fair market value of materials supplied). However, that would not be the case if, for example, the cost of unsolicited work far exceeded the enhanced value of the property.

Lusty v Finsbury Securities Ltd (1992)

The claimant was an architect employed by the defendant property owners in connection with the construction of an office block. The defendant revised the scheme, and the claimant agreed to submit drawings for revised scheme. He told the defendant that the cost would be about £2,000. The claimant was not paid for the revised drawings. The scheme was never built. The claimant's contention that there was an agreement to pay the extra £2,000, to which the defendants had consented by their silence, failed. However, the trial judge gave judgment for the claimant, holding that there was a new contract for extra work and a *quantum meruit* was £2,300. On appeal, it was held that the claimant's evidence as to the value of his work was admissible (that he was an interested party went only to the weight of his evidence). If every time a professional man sued for his fees he had to have some independent evidence for what he himself considered to be his proper fees, it would clearly be intolerable. He must be fully entitled to give his own view to the court and to see whether the court accepts that view of what is the proper sum to be awarded for the fees which he proposed to charge.

Laserbore Ltd v Morrison Biggs Wall Ltd (1993)

The claimants were microtunnelling experts, employed by the defendants as subcontractors. There was a simple contract which contained an express terms providing that the defendants 'reimburse' the claimant 'fair and reasonable payment'. The claimant's expert attempted to assess reasonable rates. The defendant's expert considered the matter on a costs-plus basis. The Court preferred to ask the question, 'What would be a fair commercial rate for the services provided?' and, thus, that the reasonable rates approach more closely answered this question.

Costs-plus was considered the wrong approach 'in principle', which conclusion the Court tested by asking whether, if a company's directors are sufficiently canny to buy materials at knockdown prices from a liquidator, must they pass on this benefit? Similarly, if an expensive item of equipment has been depreciated to nothing in the company's accounts, but by careful maintenance the company continues to use it, must the equipment be provided free of charge? A costs-plus basis would answer these questions 'yes', which is not correct.

Banque Paribas v Venaglass (1994)

The claimant entered into an agreement with a developer for the redevelopment of a site it owned. The developer ran into financial difficulties, following which the claimant terminated the agreement. The work carried out had to be valued by an independent third party. The bank was the assignee of the developer's interest in the agreement. The bank argued that the value of the work required reasonable remuneration for the work done. The claimant contented that the value of the works should be assessed by reference to the open market value of the site as was attributable to the work done. The Court of Appeal agreed with the bank, and held that it was the valuation of the work done and materials supplied that was to be ascertained. The independent third party would be entitled to refer to the prices in the actual building contract between the developer and the building contractor, insofar as he considered it would assist.

Costain Civil Engineering Ltd and another v Zanen Dredging and Contracting Company Ltd (1996)

See above for the facts. The sum awarded by the arbitrator having found an entitlement to a *quantum meruit* for additional work outside the scope of the subcontract, was assessed at £370,756 plus on costs for the work done; and a sum of £386,000 in respect of the subcontractor's share of the profit arising from the works to the marina. The Court was asked whether the determination of the *quantum meruit* could properly be valued by reference to any profit allegedly made by the joint venture and/or by reference to charges (such as the costs of mobilisation and demobilisation), which a competitor for the said work would have incurred but which the subcontractor in the circumstances would not have incurred. Alternatively, was the determination confined to the value of work done and the materials supplied with a fair and reasonable percentage uplift in respect of overheads and profit?

The Court held that the approaches above were not mutually exclusive but were all elements that could be taken into consideration by the arbitrator in arriving at his judgment as to what was fair and reasonable. The question for the Court was whether or not the arbitrator gave such undue weight to any of the elements that the approach was demonstrably wrong. This was answered in the negative.

Sanjay Lachhani v Destination Canada (UK) Ltd (1997)

The defendants required extensive work to their offices. They engaged architects to prepare drawings and a specification, and let the strip-out works to a Mr Vaghjiani. The latter in fact engaged others to carry out the works, invoicing the defendants in the name of Jupiter Builders. The defendants then approached Mr Vaghjiani to tender for the main work, who in turn approached the claimants allowing them to believe that he was a representative of the defendants. The claimants and the defendants considered that there was a contract in place for the work in the sum of £100,000. The work took longer than anticipated and there were additional works. It was decided that no contract had in fact been concluded. The issue was therefore the basis of remuneration. Mr Recorder Reese QC found that when fixing the appropriate level of remuneration, any pricing level at which the building contractor had indicated it was prepared to undertake the works ought to be taken into account. A building contractor ought not be better off as a result of the failure to conclude a contract than he would have been if his offer had been accepted.

Thus, in some cases it may well be appropriate to take into account established market prices. In other cases it may well be appropriate to consider the level or levels of prices at which the parties had been negotiating before the works were commenced. In others, although in many cases a 'fair value' may be calculated on a 'costs-plus' basis, the allowable remuneration may fall to be capped by reference to a pricing level put forward by the contractor.

Serck Controls Ltd v Drake & Scull Engineering Ltd (1997)

The claimant carried out design and installation work for the defendant, as part of the construction of a replacement research and development facility for British Nuclear Fuels Ltd. The basis of the quantum trial was that the claimant was entitled to be paid on a *quantum meruit* basis, there having been no concluded contract between the parties. HHJ Hicks QC considered that:

> 'A *quantum meruit* claim may...arise in wide variety of circumstances, across a spectrum which ranges at one end from an express contract to do work at an unquantified price, which expressly or by implication must then be a reasonable one, to work (at the other extreme) done by an uninvited intruder which nevertheless confers on the recipient a benefit which for some reason, such as estoppel or acquiescence, it is unjust for him to retain without making restitution to the provider....At the first end of the spectrum...the measure should clearly be the reasonable remuneration of the claimant; at the other it should be the value to the defendant. In between there is a borderline, the position of which may be debatable.'

The circumstances in which the work was carried out, including the site conditions and the conduct of the other party, may be relevant to what a reasonable remuneration is.

ERDC Group Ltd v Brunel University (2006)

The claimant submitted a tender for the construction of new sports facilities at its Uxbridge campus, to be carried out on the basis of the *JCT Standard Form of Contract with Contractors Design (1998 edition)*. Pending full planning permission, progressed with the design of the works under the terms of a letter of appointment. Further letters of appointment were issued and the claimant started construction under further such letters. When the works were largely complete, the claimant declined to sign and claimed (for the first time) that it would only continue work on the basis that all work carried out by it would be valued on a quantum meruit basis rather than in accordance with the valuation principles applicable under the *JCT Standard Form of Building Contract with Contractors Design* (the *JCT Valuation Rules*). The claimant left site, by agreement, at the end of March 2003. The works were then not entirely complete.

The Court found that there was a clear intention to create legal relations, and that the work done pursuant to the letters of contract prior to the expiry of the last contract on 1 September 2002 was to be treated and valued as if it had been carried out under the contract contemplated by the last letter. It was not to be valued on a quantum meruit basis. After 1 September 2002, it was agreed that the basis of payment would be *quantum meruit*, but the claimant contended that this would be a costs-plus approach, and the defendant contended that this would mean the continuation of the contractual approach. The Court held that there are no hard and fast rules for the assessment of a quantum meruit, and all the factors have to be considered. On the facts of this case, which were unusual in that there was a move from contractual to a non-contractual basis, it was considered incorrect to switch from an assessment based on the claimant's rates to one based entirely on its costs.

1.5 PAYMENT CLAIMS UNDER THE HOUSING GRANTS, CONSTRUCTION AND REGENERATION ACT 1996

The *Housing Grants, Construction and Regeneration Act* 1996 ('the 1996 Act') affects not only the basis upon which but also the ease with which parties are able to bring claims under any contract, which meets the definition of a 'construction contract' for the purposes of the statute. The 1996 Act has given rise to a substantial body of first instance, Court of Appeal and, very recently, House of Lords authority. Many of the cases relate not to the payment provisions of the 1996 Act, but to the process of adjudication and the circumstances in which the court will enforce, or decline to enforce, the temporarily binding effect of an adjudicator's decision. These cases are outside the scope of this book. However, this chapter identifies a number of the key cases, and in particular the recent House of Lords case of *Melville v Dundas*, which deal with the interpretation and application of the payment provisions of the 1996 Act.

1.5.1 The payment provisions

The payment provisions of the 1996 Act are set out in ss. 109 to 113. Section 109 sets out a statutory entitlement to stage payments (see section 1.1 above). Section 112 provides a contractor with a statutory right to suspend performance of his obligations should amounts to which he is properly entitled under the Act remain unpaid. Section 113 prohibits, except in certain situations, those clauses which are generally know as 'pay when paid' clauses.

However, the most important of the Act are ss. 110 and 111. These state:

'**110**. – (1) Every construction contract shall-

(a) provide an adequate mechanism for determining what payments become due under the contract, and when, and

(b) provide for a final date for payment in relation to any sum which becomes due.

The parties are free to agree how long the period is to be between the date on which a sum becomes due and the final date for payment.

(2) Every construction contract shall provide for the giving of notice by a party not later than five days after the date on which a payment becomes due from him under the contract, or would have become due if-

(a) the other party had carried out his obligations under the contract, and

(b) no set-off or abatement was permitted by reference to any sum claimed to be due under one or more other contracts,

specifying the amount (if any) of the payment made or proposed to be made, and the basis on which that amount was calculated.

(3) If or to the extent that a contract does not contain such provision as is mentioned in subsection (1) or (2), the relevant provisions of the Scheme for Construction Contracts apply.

Payment claims

111. – (1) A party to a construction contract may not withhold payment after the final date for payment of a sum due under the contract unless he has given an effective notice of intention to withhold payment.

The notice mentioned in section 110(2) may suffice as a notice of intention to withhold payment if it complies with the requirements of this section.

(2) To be effective such a notice must specify-

(a) the amount proposed to be withheld and the ground for withholding payment, or

(b) if there is more than one ground, each ground and the amount attributable to it,

and must be given not later than the prescribed period before the final date for payment.

(3) The parties are free to agree what that prescribed period is to be.

In the absence of such agreement, the period shall be that provided by the Scheme for Construction Contracts.

(4) Where an effective notice of intention to withhold payment is given, but on the matter being referred to adjudication it is decided that the whole or part of the amount should be paid, the decision shall be construed as requiring payment not later than –

(a) seven days from the date of the decision, or

(b) the date which apart from the notice would have been the final date for payment,

whichever is the later.'

1.5.2 Withholding notices

Sections 110 and 111 are therefore intended to ensure that any construction contract makes clear by what mechanism it is to be determined what amounts are due and by when. In relation to any sum that has fallen due under a construction contract, the paying party cannot usually withhold payment unless a notice complying with s. 111 of the 1996 has been served within the time limits. This obviously has an effect on the ability of the paying party to resist claims at least in the short term unless he has complied with the notification requirements.

There was, until the decision of *Rupert Morgan v Jervis*, considerable uncertainty as to the meaning of s. 111 and, as will be seen in a different context, uncertainty remains following the decision of the House of Lords in *Melville v Dundas*. The first cases summarised in the chapter deal with the 'narrow' and 'broad' constructions of s. 111 and what is generally considered the 'right' construction, as clarified in *Rupert Morgan*. The earlier cases remain useful points of reference in understanding the what the nature of a withholding is, and, just as importantly, is not.

Northern Developments (Cumbria) Ltd v J & J Nichol (2000)

The Court held that the intention of the statute was that if there is to be a dispute about the amount of the payment required by s. 111, that dispute is to be mentioned in a notice of intention to withhold payment not later than five days after the due date for payment. It was considered that, for the temporary striking of balances which were contemplated by the Act, there 'was to be no dispute about any matter not raised in a notice of intention to withhold payment'. This case is considered to be the high water mark of those cases dealing with the requirement to issue a withholding notice. There are now, clearly, a number of exceptions to the general statement set out by the Court in this case.

KNS Industrial Services (Birmingham) Ltd v Sindall Ltd (2000)

A much more narrow view was expressed in this case by the Court. It was held that the term 'withhold' was used in s. 111 to cover both the situation where in arriving at a valuation the contractor had not taken account of a countervailing factor as well as the situation where there was to be reduction in or deduction from an amount that had been declared or thought to be due. In the former case the word 'withhold' may not always be correct, because one cannot withhold what is not due.

S L Timber v Carillion (2001)

Lord MacFadyen, in the Scottish Outer House, held that a 'sum due under the contract' could not be equated with a 'sum claimed'. Section 111 was declared not to be concerned with every refusal on the part of one party to pay a sum claimed by the other. Rather, the Court considered that the section was concerned with the situation where a sum is due under the contract, and the party by whom that sum is due seeks to withhold payment on some separate ground. If this were correct as a general proposition, then the employer who wished to rely upon arguments, amongst others, that (a) the work was not done at all, (b) the work was done defectively giving rise to abatement, or (c) there is no contractual entitlement for the work done, could do so without giving any notice to the contractor by way of notice of intention to withhold under s. 111. However, it has been clarified in *Rupert Morgan* (below) that whilst this is not correct by way of general proposition, it remains the correct analysis if there is no contractual mechanism (such as certified interim certificates) which determines, for the purposes of the contract, what is 'due'. Lord MacFadyen's analysis may therefore be applicable where the facts of the case are similar.

It should also be noted that *S. L. Timber* was in the context of a contract to which the Scheme applied. If, as in the *JCT With Contractor's Design 1998* standard form (but *not*, interestingly, the updated version of the standard form, the *JCT Design and Build 2005*), the amount *claimed* is, in the absence of a payment and/or withholding notice, the amount due, then the issue is much more simple. In this situation, by virtue of the contractual wording, if *any* attack is to be made on the amount claimed, the payment and/or withholding notice *must* be served.

Millers Specialist Joinery v Nobles Construction (2000)

In considering s. 111, it was decided that:
1   A withholding notice is required if the defence to payment is 'I do not have to pay this invoice/application because I have overpaid on previous invoices/applications and I therefore abate the sum you claim by the sum of this overpayment' (abatement – i.e. any abatement).

2   A withholding notice is required if the defence to payment is 'I do not have to pay this invoice/application because I am entitled to set-off sums due to me in damages or pursuant to the contract' (set-off).

3   The amount claimed in a valuation/application is not to be treated as the amount 'due under the contract' (within s. 111). A withholding notice is not required if the defence to payment is 'I do not have to pay this invoice/application because the sum you have claimed is not due under the contract' ('pure' valuation).

However, this analysis has also been effectively superceded by the clarification in *Rupert Morgan*.

Clark Contracts v The Burrell Co (2002)

The claimants were employed by the defendant as the main contractors in relation to a redevelopment of eight flats at Cleveden Drive, Glasgow. The conditions governing the contract were the *SBCC Design Portion with Quantities (September 1997 Revision) Building Contract with Scottish Supplement 1980 (Revised, July 1997)* to the *Conditions of the Standard Form of Building Contract 1980 edition with Quantities*. Interim Certificate No. 11 in the gross amount of £486,529.42 was issued and following the issue of previous certificates the defendant had made payment to the claimants of the sum of £451,529.42. Net of retention the sum certified by Interim Certificate No. 11 was £28,525, which together with VAT made the sum brought out in the certificate to be £29,408. In their pleaded case, the claimants relied upon the interim certificate as their entitlement to payment, and did not specify the works which they had performed and which underpinned their claim which had resulted in Interim Certificate No. 11 being issued. It was held that the claimants became entitled to payment of the sum brought out in the interim certificate within 14 days of it being issued. That was an entitlement to payment of a sum due under the contract. In order to reach the figure in the interim certificate the parties had made use of the contractual mechanism.

Rupert Morgan Building Services (LLC) Ltd v Jervis (David) and Jervis (Harriet) [CA] (2003)

Contractors were engaged by the employers to carry out building works on a cottage pursuant to the Architecture and Surveying Institute standard form. The contractors sought summary judgment for payment of certified sums. The employers disputed the claim on grounds that the works for which payment was claimed were not carried out, or had already been paid for. However, no withholding notice had been served. In considering the narrow and broad views set out in the cases summarised above, the Court of Appeal approved the distinction drawn by the court in *Clark Contracts* between a contract with a mechanism for deciding what was 'due', and a contract with no such mechanism. In *S. L. Timber*, the decision was explained by the fact that the contract in that case had no architect or system of certificates. The builder simply presented his bill for payment. The Court of Appeal explained that the bill in itself did not make any sums due. What, under such a contract, would make the sums due was just the fact of the work having been done. So, in that case, no withholding notice was necessary in respect of works not done – payment was not due in respect of them. However, the situation was different where a sum had been certified for payment. The certification itself was sufficient to give the contractor a right to payment, and if the employer was to avoid the requirement to pay a certified sum when it fell due on whatever basis, it needed to serve a withholding notice setting out that basis.

Melville Dundas Ltd (in receivership) v George Wimpey UK Ltd

Melville Dundas were employed by Wimpey. The contract was in the *JCT Standard Form with Contractors' Design (1998) edition*. On 2 May 2003 MD applied for an interim payment of £396,630. It was accepted that the sum was due and that the final date for payment was 16 May 2003. Wimpey did not pay. On 22 May 2003 MD went into receivership. They had very substantial debts. The receivers claimed payment of the sum of £396,630.

Wimpey relied on clause 27.6.5.1 of the contract, which provided that, when one party went into receivership, the provisions of this contract which required any further payment or any release or further release of retention to the contractor would not apply.

The receivers then contended that these contractual provisions were contrary to s. 111(1) of the *Housing Grants, Construction and Regeneration Act (HGCRA)* 1996. The House of Lords (3:2) allowed Wimpey's appeal against the decision of the Inner House, and decided that Wimpey was entitled to withhold the payment and that there was no conflict with the provisions of the *HGCRA 1996* such as would preclude withholding. Lord Hoffmann, doubting whether Parliament can have taken into account that parties might enter into contracts where a contractual ground for withholding payment might arise *after* the final date for payment, said that (para. 22):

> '… section 111(1) should be construed as not applying to a lawful ground for withholding payment of which it was in the nature of things not possible for notice to have been given within the statutory time frame…'

The minority view was expressed by Lord Neuberger as follows:

> '… Section 111(1) prohibits the appellant from "withhold[ing] payment …" after "the final date for payment of a sum due under the contract". … Accordingly, in so far as clause 27.6.5.1 has the effect of permitting the appellant to withhold payment of the sum, it is purporting to permit that which s. 111(1) prohibits. Therefore, to that extent, it is ineffective.'

It is as yet unclear whether this important decision by the House of Lords will be treated as one of general application (as certainly would be possible in light of the words used by Lord Hoffmann) or one which is confined more narrowly to situations of insolvency such as that in the case itself.

Pierce Design v International Ltd v Mark Johnston & another (2007)

The contract was in materially identical terms to that in *Melville Dundas*. The employer had determined the contract on the ground of failure regularly and diligently to progress the works, rather than insolvency. Further, the sums due under various interim certificates had become finally payable some months before the date of the determination. No withholding notices had been served. The Court held that *Melville Dundas* in principle applied so that the employer was not obliged to make any further payments pursuant to clause 27.6.5.1. However, the outcome of the case turned on the meaning of the proviso to clause 27.6.5.1 (not relevant, and so not substantively considered by the House of Lords). This states that clause 27.6.5.1 shall not be construed to apply to payments becoming due more than 28 days before the date of the determination *and* which the employer has unreasonably not paid. It was common ground that the payments had become due more than 28 days before the determination. The Court held that as a matter of construction of the contract, an employer would be unreasonable in not paying unless he had issued a withholding notice. It is thought that the same result would obtain in the absence of a contractual obligation to serve a withholding notice as a result of the application of s. 111 of the Act.

2
Certification

In the context of the construction industry, the nature and effect of certification is often linked intrinsically to issues about payment. Standard forms nowadays usually provide for an architect, engineer, or contract administrator to value and certify the works as they progress, although some standard forms, such as the *JCT Design and Build* (formerly known as 'With Contractor's Design'), allocate this function to the employer or employer's agent.

An important question for an contractor seeking payment is whether either approval or a certificate is required as a condition precedent to payment.

2.1 CERTIFICATES OR APPROVAL AS A CONDITION PRECEDENT TO PAYMENT

Dallman v King (1837)

The claimant was a tenant in the defendant's house. One term was that the claimant was to carry out certain works to the approval of the defendant. A separate term was that the claimant would be allowed the sum of £200 towards the alteration works, retained out of the yearly rent. It was held that the inspection and approval of the defendant was not a condition precedent to the right of the claimant to deduct the relevant amount and, moreover, if it was such a condition precedent, then it had been substantially performed. The courts will construe, if they possibly can, agreements as separate independent obligations rather than as conditions precedent.

Minster Trust v Traps Tractors (1954)

The defendant had let out earth-moving plant and machinery on hire to the claimant by a contract which provided that 'on the completion of the hire each machine will be ... reconditioned by [the claimant] ... under the supervision and to the satisfaction of the Hunt Engineering Company and the hire will cease on the issuance of their certificate that the machines have been satisfactorily overhauled on a fully reconditioned basis.' This meant that the certificate to be issued by Hunts was to be a certificate addressed to all the world, or to all who may be concerned, certifying a standard of quality extraneous to the contract.

In relation to the independence of the certifier, the Court considered that if a building owner makes the obligation of payment conditional on his architect's certificate of quality, he must not, for example, instruct his architect not to be content with less than three coats of paint, for he has impliedly undertaken that he will leave his architect free to judge independently, either by reference to the contract requirements or to his own standards of quality, whichever the case may be, how many coats of paint are required.

2.1.1 The JCT Conditions

Lubenham v South Pembrokeshire DC (1986)

The employer defendant paid the amount stated in an interim certificate, issued pursuant to the *JCT Standard Form of Contract (1963 edition)*. The claimant (who was a bondsman having elected to complete construction works in place of the contractors) contended that they were incorrect in making certain deductions for defective work and in deducting liquidated damages. The claimant withdrew from site, and the defendant served a notice of termination. It was held that the contract had been properly determined. The only obligation upon the employer was to pay the amount certified. If the contractor was unhappy with a perceived under-valuation, it could request that an appropriate adjustment be made in any subsequent certificate, or commence arbitration. Under the JCT conditions, the issue of a certificate is always a condition precedent to the right of the contractor to be paid.

Croudace v London Borough of Lambeth (1986)

The claimant agreed to construct house for the defendant under the *JCT Standard Form Local Authorities (1963 edition, July 1977 revision)*. It was common ground that the claimant's claim under the agreement for its loss and expense could not be maintained by action in the absence of a certificate from the architect.

2.1.2 The ICE Conditions

Costain Building and Civil Engineering v Scottish Rugby Union (1993)

The claimant was employed by the defendant as main contractor on the *ICE Conditions of Contract (5th edition)* for the construction of the north and south stands at Murrayfield Stadium. A certificate of completion was issued under clause 48(1) of the contract on 12 January 1993. On 10 May 1993 Costain submitted a loss and expense claim in respect of sums allegedly undercertified. As part of the claim brought, the claimant arrested the sum of £8.1m in an account of the defendant, who then applied to have the arrestment recalled on the ground that it was under no present obligation to pay the sum claimed because the engineer had declined to issue any certificate. On appeal, the Court of Session held that on the true construction of the *ICE Conditions of Contract*, a certificate of the engineer was a condition precedent to the right of the contractor to be paid.

Henry Boot Construction v Alstom Combined Cycles Ltd (2005)

The contractor was engaged by the employer in relation to the construction of a power station, the contract incorporating the *ICE Conditions of Contract (6th edition)*. Clause 60 set out the payment provisions, including the interim and final certification procedure. Work was commenced in 1994 and substantially completed in 1996. The engineer under the contract issued the final certificate on 9 October 2002. Various disputes were referred to him, including the valuation in the final certificate, and whether the contractor's claim was statute-barred under the Limitation Act 1980. The engineer decided the value of the final account, and that a certain sum was overdue for payment to the contractor.

An arbitration was commenced by the employer, seeking a review of the engineer's decision not to decide whether the contractor's claims were statute-barred. The arbitrator decided that all or almost all of the claims were statute-barred, because the relevant causes of action had arisen when the work was done or when the events on which the claims were based had occurred, between 1994 and 1996.

On appeal, it was held that on the true construction of the contract, certificates were a condition precedent to Boot's entitlement to payment under clause 60(2) and (4). They were not merely evidence of the engineer's opinion. This meant that the right to payment arose when a certificate was issued or ought to have been issued, and not earlier. However, the Court noted that it did not follow from the fact that a certificate was a condition precedent that the absence of a certificate was a bar to the right to payment. This was because the decision of the engineer in relation to certification was not conclusive of the rights of the parties, and could be reviewed by an arbitrator or by the Court.

2.2 VALIDITY OF THE CERTIFICATION PROCESS

Clearly, if upon a proper construction of the contract certification is not a condition precedent to payment, then a certificate is not required for a contractor to become entitled to payment. However, even where on the face of the contract the certificate is required prior to payment under the contract, there are circumstances which may arise entitling the contractor to payment without certificate, which include:

- the failure of the employer to put in place certifier or replace the certifier;
- the wrongful refusal or failure of the certifier to certify;

- the interference in the certification process by the employer;
- the failure of the certificate to comply with the requirements of the contract;
- the replacement of the certifier by the employer, where this is not expressly permitted by the contract;
- the replacement of the certification process by an award of the Court, arbitrator or adjudicator.

Hickman v Roberts (1913)

The contract provided that the decision of the architect in relation to matters would be final, and that payments were to be made on the architect's certification. The architect refrained from issuing an interim certicate from the months of April to June, and he did not issue his final certificate until he was directed by the solicitors of the building owner to do so. The owners could not rely upon this certificate, either as a condition precedent or as an adjudication binding on the other party. The architect had placed himself in a position which deprived his certificate of the value which otherwise it would have had.

Panamena Europea Navigacion v Leyland (1947)

A contract stipulated that payment for repairs to vessel should be effected promptly after the issue of a certificate by the owners' surveyor that the work has been satisfactorily carried out. The surveyor considered his function of certification was not confined to passing the actual quality of the work done, but that he was also entitled to consider the manner in which the work had been carried out, and, in particular, whether there had been reasonable economy in time, labour and materials. The surveyor declined to deal with the question of certification until the information asked for by him was forthcoming. This meant that an illegitimate condition precedent to any consideration of the granting of a certificate was insisted on by the surveyor. The Court held that 'it is almost unnecessary to cite authority to establish that such conduct ... absolved the respondents from the necessity of obtaining such a certificate, and that the respondents are entitled to recover the amount claimed in the action.'

Perini Corporation v Commonwealth of Australia (1969)

The claimant had contracted with the defendant to carry out certain building works. By the contract, an official of the defendant called the Director of Works was held by the Court to be appointed as a certifier under the contract. Disputes arose between the parties in relation to the claimant's applications for extensions of time. It was held that there was an implied term in the contract that the defendant would not interfere with the Director of Works' duties as certifier.

Croudace v London Borough of Lambeth (1986)

The absence of the certificate was itself caused by the breach of an implied obligation upon the employer to nominate a replacement for the architect when he had retired. The failure to take such steps as were necessary to enable the contractor's claim for loss and expense to be ascertained caused the contractor loss in the sum which would have been ascertained. Whilst therefore the contractor did not have a claim for payment under the contract, it had a claim for loss and damage for breach of it.

Construction Award No 3 (1994)

In this arbitration award (in relation to which Mr John Dyson QC sat as legal assessor), the arbitrator considered the assumed scenario where events had occurred such as to entitle the contractor to an extension of time under clause 23 and loss and expense under clause 24 of the *JCT Standard Form (1963 edition)*. However, the architect had failed to grant an extension of time or certify loss and expense, not because he had come to a decision against the contractor on the merits, nor because he had not yet felt able to come to a decision one way or the other on the merits, but because had simply failed to consider the matter at all. Such a failure to deal is a breach of contract: the employer who maintains in place an architect who simply ignores without consideration claims by contractors for extension of time and loss and expense is as much in breach of contract as is an employer (as in *Croudace*, above) who fails to keep in place an architect at all.

Birse Construction Ltd v Co-operative Wholesale Society (1997)

The appellant contractor was engaged for the construction of a shopping centre. under the 1963 edition of the *JCT Standard Form of Building Contract*. The respondent was the nominated mechanical and electrical services subcontractor under the so called 'Green Form', which is designed for use where a subcontractor is nominated by the architect under the *JCT Form*. After completion of the contract work, disputes arose under both the main contract and the subcontract. In an arbitration under the main contract, the arbitrator found that events that were not the responsibility of the main contractor or the subcontractor had caused delay and disruption causing substantial loss and expense including moneys claimed by the subcontractor. The employer did not honour the award. The subcontractor claimed to be entitled, without further proof, to recover amounts in question from the main contractor in an arbitration under the subcontract. The Court of Appeal held that it was implicit where, in an arbitration under the main contract, a tribunal makes an award of a sum which should have been certified as due in respect of the subcontract works, that sum falls to be treated in the subcontract as a sum duly certified, so that, in that respect, the award is binding in the subcontract.

BR & EP Cantrell v Wright & Fuller Ltd (2003)

The claimant employers contracted with the defendant under the *JCT Standard Conditions of Contract (1980 edition)*. The works achieved practical completion on 23 February 1998. On 12 March 1999 the architect sent the claimants the final account and an interim certificate (dated 10 March 1999) for an interim payment in the sum of approximately £25,000. On 29 March 1999 the architect produced a certificate that the respondents relied upon as being the final certificate. In the arbitration, there was a dispute as to whether this was a final certificate within the meaning of clause 30.8. The Court held that:

- The certificate must be:
    - one which clearly expresses the relevant opinion of the architect in a form that shows that the opinion is that of the architect;

Certification

- one which the contract calls for; and
- one which addresses and only addresses the matters called for.

- If the certificate is, on its face, clear and unambiguous, there will be little or no need to consider extraneous contemporary material in order to be satisfied that it fulfils the form, substance and intent test.
- Where the certificate is itself ambiguous, recourse may be made to any covering letter or other contemporaneous document which was produced with or as part of the certifying process so long as that additional document is properly to be regarded as being issued as part of the certificate.
- If it is contended that the certificate was not the product of the architect and therefore not an expression of his own intent, additional evidence will be both admissible and required.

The document issued on 29 March 1999 was declared not to be the final certificate in either form, substance or intent.

Scheldebouw BV v St James Homes (Grosvenor Dock) Ltd (2006)

The issue arose as to whether or not the employer could appoint itself as the replacement construction manager who, under the construction management form of procurement, had 'decision-making' functions on matters where, at least potentially, the contractor and the employer have opposing interests (such as the certification of loss and expense payable, adjustments to the contract sum on account of instructions and in relation to extensions of time). The Court held that it could not. It was considered such an unusual state of affairs for the employer himself to be the certifier and decision-maker that this could only be achieved by an express term. In every authority in which the certifier was a direct employee of the employer, this circumstance was known to the contractor at the outset. The contractor thus went into such a contract with his eyes open.

It is relevant to note that allowing interference in a certificate not only has the potential to invalidate the certificate, and give a claim for breach of contract against the employer, but may in principle give rise to a cause of action against the architect.

John Mowlem & Co PLC v Eagle Star Insurance Co Ltd & Others (1993)

The claimants were management contractors for a developer in relation to a site in London. The fourth defendant, PRP, was the architect. In arbitration proceedings, the claimants had succeeded in recovering substantial damages for wrongful termination of the contract against the developer; these sums were not paid. The claimants then commenced litigation against the defendants to recover, in tort, the amount claimed in the arbitration. One of the claims against PRP was that they failed to act independently of the developer and did not exercise any proper or independent judgment in deciding whether to issue the certificates and deliberately misapplied the provisions of the contract with the intention of depriving the claimant of the sums to which they were contractually entitled. In these circumstances it was claimed that PRP knowingly and wrongfully interfered with performance of the management contract and procured or facilitated a breach of the management contract by the developer. The application to have these claims struck out as disclosing no reasonable cause of action was dismissed.

2.3   CAN CERTIFICATES BE BINDING?

Where the contract provides clearly, the certificate of an architect or engineer or any authorised certifier can have a binding effect. This will therefore dictate the extent of any payment claim, or indeed, the extent to which an employer could argue that a lesser sum is to be paid. The binding effect of a certificate can also affect extension of time or loss and expense claims (considered later in this book).

It is essential that a party follows any contractual procedure laid down to prevent a certificate becoming binding if it is to be challenged. Often, the binding effect will be limited if one or other party commences dispute resolution procedures within a certain period of time of the issue of certificate.

A conclusive certificate will also usually have a significant effect upon the employer's ability to bring a claim for defects in the work. Many of the certification cases relate more to this question than to contractor's payment claims. The relevant cases are considered in section 2.12 of *Building Defects,* and section 6.1 in *Contract Administration*, other books in the *Case in Point* series.

3
Variation claims

A variation claim is a claim by a contractor for additional payment. Such a claim generally arises because the scope of the work has changed. Problems frequency arise because:

- the parties cannot agree what work was required by the original scope required;
- there is a dispute as to whether any additional work was instructed;
- contractual notice provisions have not been complied with before work is carried out;
- neither party can agree how much the additional work should be valued at.

Most standard-form building contracts make express provision for a mechanism to determine whether and what additional cost can be recovered. The mechanisms are aimed at avoiding or at least minimising the type of disagreements identified above. However, it is invariably the case that contractual procedures are ignored or misapplied and, even if applied, do not prevent fundamental disagreements arising out of a different perception of the contractual obligations.

3.1 WHAT IS A VARIATION?

The starting point for defining additional work is to understand the original scope of work.

In a contract to complete a project for a lump sum, the court will often conclude that the contractor has promised to provide everything necessary to carry out the project.

Williams v Fitzmaurice (1858)

The claimant was contracted to build a house for the defendant. The obligation was that the house was 'to be dry and fit for ... occupation' and the claimant was to provide 'the whole of the materials ... necessary for the completion of the work'. The specification did not include flooring and the claimant refused to supply it without additional payment. The defendant terminated the contract. The Court held that the claimant could not recover either the amount outstanding or the cost of the floorboards, which the defendant had seized upon taking over the site. The words used in the contract clearly inferred that flooring was necessary to complete the house.

Sharpe v San Paulo Railways (1873)

The contractor engaged to build a railway in Brazil undertook to complete the whole line, with everything that was requisite for the purpose of completion, from the beginning to the end for a lump sum. The engineer's original plans were inadequate, and vastly underestimated the amount of excavation required. Nevertheless, the contractor was held liable to complete all the work as part of the original lump sum. It was held that the amount of excavation was a thing the contractors ought to have looked at for themselves and made out their own calculations.

It should be noted, of course, that as a matter of construction in this particular contract, the engineer's plans did not override the principal obligation to build the railway line. It may be that an differently worded obligation (e.g. 'build the railway in accordance with the engineer's plans') would have given rise to the risk of inadequacy of the engineer's plans falling upon the employer. Modern standard forms will attempt to allocate the risk as between the parties for the information/plans provided by the employer for carrying out the work.

Bottoms v York Corp (1892)

The claimant contractor was engaged to build a sewerage system. No soil tests or trial holes were carried out prior to tender. The contract contained no undertaking in respect of the soil in which the sewer was to be constructed. The contractor's tender was £10,000 lower than the other lowest tenderer, no doubt because of the claimant's 'very superficial view of the nature of the soil...'. The defendants 'allowed themselves to be tempted to accept the tender... what no one of the highly respectable gentlemen of whom the Corporation was composed would have done if the matter concerned himself only; but Corporations are popular institutions, because they are not afflicted with the qualms of conscience....' Nevertheless, when the soil conditions turned out in fact to be of such character as required extensive shuttering, no claim for a variation succeeded.

Leedsford v City of Bradford (1956)

The claimant contracted with the defendant council to construct a new infants' school. The contract provided for the use of 'Artificial Stone ... The following to be obtained from the Empire Stone Company Limited ... or other approved firm ...' The architect refused to give his consent to artificial stone being obtained from the companies proposed by the claimant. The claimant's claim for the additional cost of providing stone from Empire Stone over and above the cost of supply from its own proposed supplier failed. According to the Court of Appeal, the term in the contract meant that the stone was to be Empire Stone unless the parties both agreed some other stone, and that no other stone could be substituted except by mutual agreement. It was open to the architect to refuse to approve any other stone, providing he was acting in good faith.

Neodox v Swinton and Pendlebury BC (1958)

The claimant contracted to construct sewage works for the defendant council. The contract gave to the engineer the power to determine the method by which works were to be executed, such as the excavation of trenches where alternative methods were possible. The Court found that whilst the engineer's decision as to whether one method or another is satisfactory to him must be an honest one, the defendant did not warrant his competency or skill, or warrant that his decision would be reasonable. Diplock J considered that in a contract in which there was no specific method of carrying out particular operations necessary to complete the works set out, and which provided merely that they should be carried out under the engineer's directions and in the best manner to his satisfaction, it was difficult to see how a direction by the engineer intimating the manner in which the operations must be carried out in order to satisfy him could be a 'variation of or addition to the works'.

Canterbury Pipe Lines Ltd v Christchurch Drainage Board (1979)

The defendant engaged the claimant to construct a sewer, involving excavation, laying pipes, backfilling and replacing the road surface. Work started, but with the acquiescence of the Board there was then a delay pending delivery to the contractor of a piece of heavy-duty trenching equipment, called a Parsons trenchliner. Once available, this machine was expected to enable the contract to be completed more expeditiously. In the event its advantage in that respect proved to be accompanied by the disadvantage that more backfill had to be imported. The claimant's claim for additional payment in relation to the imported backfill failed. The Court held that because the contract did not lay down the manner in which the claimant had to make the excavations, and it was therefore left to the claimant to decide on matters of technique, there was no reason that the additional cost should be borne by the defendant.

Bills of quantities usually feature as an essential element of a remeasurement contract. A 'change' in estimated quantities in a remeasurement contract is not a variation – it is merely part of the work for which payment is made in accordance with the terms of the contract. However, a bill of quantities is sometimes included as part of a lump sum contract in order to describe more particularly the works to be carried out. If the bill of quantities forms part of the contract, work additional to the quantities shown can constitute a variation. It is a matter of construction whether the bill forms part of the contract, in this way, or simply part of the information provided for the purposes of the tender.

Patman and Fotheringham v Pilditch (1904)

The claimant contractors were engaged by the defendant to construct a block of flats 'according to plans ... and bills of quantities ...' which had been prepared by the defendant. A term of the contract provided that, 'the contractors shall supply everything of every sort and kind which may be necessary and requisite for the due and proper execution of the ... works.' The estimate of quantities was wrong in such a way as would (had the proper quantities been provided) have affected the contract price. The Court held that the quantities were introduced into the contract as part of the description of the work, and that therefore, if the contractor is required, in order to complete the work, to do more than is in the quantities, he is entitled to have that as extra.

3.2 INSTRUCTIONS

Variations often arise out of instructions. The courts have considered the power of architects or surveyors to issue instructions which bind the employer.

Sharpe v San Paulo Railway (1873)

See above for the facts. One of the arguments raised by the claimants was that the defendant was bound by the (apparently vague) assurances of the engineer in relation to what was claimed to be the additional work. The Court held, finding that the work was part of the original scope, that it was in any event quite clear that the engineer had no power to vary the contract; he had power to give directions to do certain things upon the line within the limits of the contract. If the contractors thought that these things were not within the contract they were not bound to do them. The claimants could not therefore 'vary the contract and make a new and substituted contract by reason of any conversations said to have been held with the engineer'.

Carlton Contractors v Bexley Corp (1962)

The claimant contractors agreed to build 112 houses for the defendant. During the negotiations, discrepancies were discovered between the bill of quantities and the drawings, and various changes were allegedly agreed prior to signing the contract, between the claimant and the borough's surveyor (who was the architect for the works). The contract did not contain these changes. It was held, on a claim for rectification, that the borough surveyor was in a position to negotiate the terms of the arrangement and the claimant was entitled to rely upon legal effect given to the agreement as part of the intention common to both side. The borough surveyor was acting within his ostensible authority to bind the corporation.

Stockport MBC v O'Reilly (1978)

O'Reilly entered into a contract with the claimant to build 105 houses. The agreement provided for a completion date in November 1969. The architect sought to impose phases in place of dates and gave directions to employ certain people on particular parts of the work. These instructions, and others, were not empowered by any of the conditions of the contract. It was held that an architect's *ultra vires* acts do not saddle the employer with liability. 'The architect is not the employer's agent in that respect. He has no authority to vary the contract.' If the parties acquiesce in the instruction the contract may be *pro tanto* varied and then the acts cannot be complained of. However, the contractor is entitled to protest and to ignore them. Either way, the contractor cannot saddle the employer with responsibility for them.

3.3 RELIANCE UPON INFORMATION PROVIDED BY THE EMPLOYER

Often, variation claims arise out of conditions which differ from those presented on drawings or other data provided for the purposes of tendering by the employer. However, there is no implied warranty as to the accuracy of the information so as to give rise automatically to a claim for additional payment.

Thorn v London Corp (1876)

The claimant contracted with the defendant to take down the old Blackfriars Bridge and build a new one, having been supplied with plans and a specification. The descriptions were stated as 'believed to be correct', but were not guaranteed. The plan required the use of caissons, but once put in, it was found that these were of no use. The claimant sought compensation by way of a variation clause for his loss of time and labour caused by the failure of the caissons. It was held that no warranty as to the accuracy of the information was intended or implied, and that 'if there is no express warranty, your Lordships cannot imply a warranty, unless from the circumstances of the work some warranty must have been necessary, which clearly is not the case here.' Therefore it was down to the claimant contractor to take precautions, whether by express warranty or by independent investigations, to protect itself from any loss.

Tharsis Sulphur & Copper Company v McElroy & Sons (1878)

The claimant contractor found that it was unable to make certain girders, due to the thinness of the metal specified by the defendant. It was held by the House of Lords that the claimant had taken the risk of being able to make the girders of the specified dimensions, and because there was no express instruction by the defendant's engineers to make the girders of a thicker metal, the extra cost could not be recovered.

Bacal Construction (Midlands) Ltd v The Northampton Development Corporation (1975)

The claimant contractor had prepared foundation designs on the assumption that the soil conditions were as shown on the data provided by the defendant employer. There was a further, express statement in the tender documentation that the soil was of a particular type. During the works, different soil conditions were discovered, necessitating a redesign and additional work. The claimant contended that it was an implied term of the contract that the ground conditions would accord with the data given to it. The Court of Appeal agreed, relying on the express words of the contract (which did not provide for additional payment for this additional work) to imply a warranty on the basis that the parties must have intended it.

Variation claims

3.4 OMISSION OF WORK

Although a contract may give power to the employer or architect to omit work, it may well be that there is, upon a proper construction, no power to omit work with the intention of giving that work to another party.

AMEC Building Ltd v Cadmus Investment Company (1996)

In a contract between AMEC and Cadmus, certain fitting-out works were covered by provisional sums in the original contract sum. The architect instructed that the fitting-out work was to be omitted from AMEC's contract. Subsequently the work was let to another contractor. AMEC claimed loss of profit. It was argued on behalf of Cadmus that the contract entitled the architect to omit parts of the work covered by provisional sums, even if it is intended to give it to a third party. Cadmus also relied upon alleged good reasons for its decision, although these reasons had been rejected as a matter of fact by the arbitrator. On appeal from the arbitrator's award, the Court held that without a finding that the architect was entitled to withdraw the work for the reasons advanced by Cadmus, the only conclusion that the Court could come to was that the withdrawal of work had been arbitrary and, in those circumstances, was something for which AMEC was entitled to be compensated. By inference, this case suggests that if Cadmus had established valid reasons for the withdrawal of work, not withstanding the fact it was then given to a third party, AMEC's claim may have failed.

Abbey Developments Ltd v PP Brickwork Ltd (2003)

Abbey engaged PPB as a labour-only subcontractor for brickwork and blockwork. Clause 2 of the subcontract conditions empowered Abbey to increase or reduce the quantity of work. The question was whether this enabled the employer to determine the entire subcontract.

The Court considered that a contract for the execution of work confers on the contractor not only the duty to carry out the work, but the corresponding right to be able to complete the work which it contracted to carry out. The work has to be defined for there to be a right to execute it. To take away or to

51

vary the work is to be considered an intrusion into and an infringement of that right and a breach of contract. Hence, contracts contain provisions to enable the employer to vary the work in order to achieve lawfully what could be achieved without breaking the contract or by a separate further agreement with the contractor. By entering into a contract with a variations clause, such further agreement is obviated, as the contractor's consent to changes in the work is in the primary contract.

However, the Court considered that provisions entitling an owner to vary the work have to be construed carefully so as not to deprive the contractor of its contractual right to the opportunity to complete the works and realise such profit as may then be made. Reasonably clear words are needed in order to remove work from the contractor simply to have it done by somebody else, whether because the prospect of having it completed by the contractor will be more expensive for the employer than having it done by somebody else, although there can well be other reasons such as timing and confidence in the original contractor.

Trustees of Stratfield Saye Estate v AHL Construction Ltd (2004)

The claimant estate owned a derelict property. It entered into a contract with a local builder to make the building weathertight. The works could only be generally described and an agreement was reached on a costs-plus basis, with agreed rates. AHL duly set up on site and started work, although one week later the estate cancelled the project. AHL commenced a number of adjudications, the third of which sought compensation for cancellation of the project. These losses were awarded. In the course of giving judgment in respect of the enforceability of the third adjudication award, the Court considered whether there was a contract for a defined scope of work. Approving the principles laid down in *Abbey*, the Court held that the employer was fully entitled to give instructions which would vary the details set out on the drawings or the works described in the site minutes. However, the employer's power to omit works was subject to a clear limit. AHL had been employed to carry out the works which would convert the derelict property into a building which was weathertight. The employer had no power to

3.5 CONDITIONS PRECEDENT TO CLAIMING FOR ADDITIONAL WORK

Construction contracts will often contain clauses requiring a contractor to notify the employer of events which may entitle him to additional payment under the contract. In general, the courts have taken a strict approach when faced with such notice requirements, finding them to be conditions precedent which must be satisfied before a contractor can hope to bring a successful variation claim. Where a contractor fails to comply with such a clause, he may therefore be deprived of a remedy. This strict approach is taken so that the employer is able to consider the situation and it financial implications. (See *Hudson's Building Contracts* (4th edition) Vol. 2, p.565.)

Tersons Ltd v Stevenage Development Corporation (1963)

Under clause 52(2) of the *ICE Conditions of Contract (4th edition)*, a contractor was obliged to give notice in writing to the defendant's engineer when claiming extra payment. Under clause 52(4), the contractor was further required to give notice to the engineer on a monthly basis of any additional expense claimed. Some six months after receiving a drawing, the contractor gave notice of its intention to seek additional payment. The Court of Appeal upheld the arbitrator's decision that compliance with clause 52 was a condition precedent to any variation and that even though no monthly notice was ever given, the contractor had given adequate notice on this particular occasion by doing so as soon as was practicable.

Hersent Offshore SA and Amsterdamse Ballast Betonen Waterbouw BV v Burmah Oil Tankers Ltd (1978)

In considering a claim arising out of an agreement for the construction of a crude oil transhipment terminal which was in substantially the same form as in *Tersons Ltd v Stevenage Development Corporation*, it was held that 'unless the claimants could excuse failure of compliance on the ground of waiver, they had to conform to the requirements of the final proviso of clause 52 as to giving notice of intention to claim extra payment.'

Jennings Construction v Birt (1986)

In this Australian case, a contract provided that the contractor was not to be liable for any variation claim unless written notice was given 'not later than 14 days after the date of the occurrence of events or circumstances on which the claim is based.' When material excavated from embankments required a specific, more expensive method of processing, the claimant contractor argued that it was entitled to additional payment despite failing to give notice within the required period. The Court identified the underlying purpose of the clause as being to enable the employer to investigate the claim and consider his position. Therefore the obligation was a strict one and the claim failed.

Wormald Engineering Ltd v Resources Conservation International (1988)

In a further Australian case, the contractor failed to give notice to the employer after a variation order, as required under the contract. The contractor was paid for some of the costs occasioned by the variation by the employer, but subsequently claimed for delay and disruption. It was held, for reasons similar to those in *Jennings Construction v Birt*, that the giving of notice was a condition precedent to any entitlement for additional payment.

In view of this uncompromising approach, contractors should pay particular attention to contractual notification provisions. The main standard form contracts provide for different notification regimes with which it is important to be familiar.

3.5.1 The JCT Standard Form of Building Contract with quantities (2005 edition)

The *JCT Standard Form* does not impose any restrictive requirement on the contractor to notify the employer, except for the 'long-stop' obligation in clause 4.5. This requires the contractor to provide the contract administrator with all documents relevant to the final adjustment of the contract sum

Variation claims

within six months of practical completion. This includes, pursuant to clauses 4.2 and 4.3, amounts payable for variations to the works:

> '**4.5** .1 Not later than 6 months after the issue by the Architect/Contract Administrator of the Practical Completion Certificate or the last Section Completion Certificate, the Contractor shall provide the Architect/Contract Administrator or (if so instructed) the Quantity Surveyor, with all documents necessary for the purposes of the adjustment of the Contract Sum.
>
> .2 Not later than 3 months after receipt by the Architect/Contract Administrator or by the Quantity Surveyor of the documents referred to in clause 4.5.1:
>
>> .1 the Architect/Contract Administrator, or, if the Architect/Contract Administrator has so instructed, the Quantity Surveyor, shall (unless previously ascertained) ascertain the amount of any loss and/or expense under clause 3.24 or 4.23; and
>>
>> .2 the Quantity Surveyor shall prepare a statement of all adjustments to be made to the Contract Sum pursuant to clause 4.3, other than the amount of any loss and/or expense then being ascertained under clause 4.5.2.1,
>
> and the Architect/Contract Administrator shall forthwith send to the Contractor a copy of that statement and (if applicable) that ascertainment.'

Clauses from the JCT Standard Form of Building Contract with quantities (2005 edition) by the Joint Contracts Tribunal Limited, Sweet & Maxwell, © The Joint Contracts Tribunal Limited, are reproduced here with permission.

Practically speaking, this entails that variation claims will be dealt with on an ongoing basis (through the interim valuation process) or at the end of the contract, once the contractor has provided the contract administrator with all of the information needed to make the final adjustment. It is therefore highly unlikely that the contractor will be deprived of a variation claim by a failure to notify.

3.5.2 The ICE Form of Contract (7th edition)

The *ICE Form of Contract* is more restrictive in its notification requirements.

Firstly, clause 52(5) provides that where a contractor considers any rate or price to be unreasonable as a result of a variation, the contractor must give the engineer notice before the varied work is commenced. This is a condition precedent (*Keating on Construction Contracts* (8th edition), p.1048).

> '**52** (5) If in the opinion of the Engineer or the Contractor any rate or price contained in the Contract for any item of work (not being the subject of any variation) is by reason of any variation rendered unreasonable or inapplicable either the Engineer shall give to the Contractor or the Contractor shall give to the Engineer notice before the varied work is commenced or as soon thereafter as is reasonable in all the circumstances that such rate or price should be increased or decreased and the Engineer shall fix such rate or price as in the circumstances he shall think reasonable and proper and shall so notify the Contractor.'

Secondly, and more broadly, clause 53 requires the contractor to notify the engineer of any variation claim as soon as is reasonable and in any case within 28 days of the event giving rise to the claim (*Keating on Construction Contracts* (8th edition), p.1048).

> '**53** (1) If the Contractor intends to claim a higher rate than one notified to him by the Engineer pursuant to sub-clauses (3) and (4) of Clause 52 or Clause 56(2) he shall give notice in writing of his intention to the Engineer.
>
> (2) If the Contractor intends to claim any additional payment pursuant to any Clause of these conditions other than sub-clauses (3) and (4) of Clause 52 or Clause 56(2) he shall give notice in writing of his intention to the Engineer as soon as may be reasonable and in any event within 28 days after the happening of the events giving rise to the claim.
>
> Upon the happening of such events the Contractor shall keep such contemporary records as may reasonably be necessary to support any claim he may subsequently wish to make.'

Variation claims

Further procedural steps with which the contractor may have to comply on instruction by the Engineer are contained in clause 53(3) and 53(4):

'(3) Without necessarily admitting the Employer's liability the Engineer may upon receipt of a notice under this Clause instruct the Contractor to keep such contemporary records or further contemporary records as the case may be as are reasonable and may be material to the claim of which notice has been given and the Contractor shall keep such records.

The Contractor shall permit the Engineer to inspect all records kept pursuant to clause 53 and shall supply him with copies thereof as and when the Engineer shall so instruct.

(4) After the giving of a notice to the Engineer under this Clause the Contractor shall as soon as is reasonable in all the circumstances send to the Engineer a first interim account giving full and detailed particulars of the amount claimed to that date and of the grounds upon which the claim is based.

Thereafter at such intervals as the Engineer may reasonably require the Contractor shall send to the Engineer further up to date accounts giving the accumulated total of the claim and any further grounds upon which it is based.'

Clause 53(6) elaborates further, stating that for claims to be accounted for in interim payments the contractor must provide sufficient particulars. Finally, and perhaps most importantly, clause 53(5) provides that where the contractor has failed to comply with the procedure in clauses 53(1) to 53(4), payment will only be made to the extent that the engineer has not been prejudiced:

'(5) If the Contractor fails to comply with any of the provisions of this Clause in respect of any claim which he shall seek to make then the Contractor shall be entitled to payment in respect thereof only to the extent that the Engineer has not been prevented from or substantially prejudiced by such failure in investigating the said claim.

(6) The Contractor shall be entitled to have included in any interim payment certified by the Engineer pursuant to Clause

60 such amount in respect of any claim as the Engineer may consider due to the Contractor provided that the Contractor shall have supplied sufficient particulars to enable the Engineer to determine the amount due.

If such particulars are insufficient to substantiate the whole of the claim the Contractor shall be entitled to payment in respect of such part of the claim as the particulars may substantiate to the satisfaction of the Engineer.'

Clauses from the ICE Conditions of Contract (7th edition), published by Thomas Telford and the Institution of Civil Engineers, are reproduced with permission.

The notification procedure under the *ICE Form of Contract (7th edition)* may therefore be summarised as follows.

1. For additional payment to be included in any interim payment, the contractor should provide sufficient particulars of his claim when notifying the engineer in writing within 28 days of the relevant event: 53(2).

2. Once the contractor has given notice, he should follow it up with a fully particularised interim account. If full particulars are not given, an appropriate level of payment may be withheld: 53(6).

3. The contractor should evidence his claim with contemporary records and may be required to do so by the engineer. The engineer may also request up-to-date accounts: 53(2), (3), (4).

4. Where the notification procedure is not followed and an inability to investigate the contractor's entitlement has prejudiced the engineer, then for the purposes of any interim or final account the engineer may withhold payment: 53(5).

5. Where a variation makes a price or rate unreasonable, the contractor should give notice to the engineer before commencing the work, if possible: 52(5).

3.5.3 The NEC Contract ECC3

Under the *NEC Contract ECC3*, the contractor may receive additional payment through the compensation event regime contained in core clause 6. The list of compensation events is contained in clause 60.1 and includes:

Variation claims

'(1) The Project Manager gives an instruction changing the Works Information except

- A change made in order to accept a Defect or

- A change to the Works Information provided by the Contractor for his design which is made either at his request or to comply with other Works Information provided by the Employer.

...

(14) An event which is an Employer's risk stated in the contract.

...

(19) An event which

- Stops the Contractor completing the works or

- Stops the Contractor completing the works by the date shown

and which

- Neither Party could prevent,

- An experienced contractor would have judged at the Contract Date to have such a small chance of occurring that it would have been unreasonable for him to have allowed it and

- Is not one of the other compensation events stated in this contract.'

Clause 60.2 also provides, notably, that:

'In judging the physical conditions for the purpose of assessing a compensation event, the Contractor is assumed to have taken into account:

- The Site Information,

- Publicly available information referred to in the Site Information,

- Information obtainable from a visual inspection of the Site and

- Other information which an experienced contractor could reasonably be expected to have or to obtain.'

As to the timing of the notification of a compensation event, clause 60.3 provides as follows:

'If the contractor does not notify a compensation event within eight weeks of becoming aware of the event, he is not entitled to a change in the prices, the completion date or a key date unless the project manager should have notified the event to the contractor but did not.'

Clause 63.4 also expressly limits the remedies available to the contractor on notifying of a compensation event:

'The rights of the employer and the contractor to changes to the prices, the completion date and the key dates are their only rights in respect of a compensation event.'

Clauses from the NEC3 Engineering and Construction Contract are reproduced here with permission from NEC Contracts.

A contractor can bring a variation claim by the following route:

1. the contractor must notify the project manager of a compensation event within eight weeks of its occurring;
2. once the compensation event has been notified the project manager invites the contractor to give a quotation for the compensation event;
3. the contractor provides its quotation;
4. the project manager either accepts the contractor's quotation, instructs the contractor to submit a revised quotation, or makes its own assessment of the effect of the compensation event in terms of time and money.

For completeness, it should also be noted that the *NEC Contract ECC3* is relatively prescriptive as to the form of any notification, requiring that the notification should be in a form which can be read, copied and recorded (13.1) and that it should be communicated separately from other communications (13.7).

4
Time for completion and extensions of time

4.1 INTRODUCTION

Even with the best will in the world, construction projects often fall into delay. This is especially so in the case of complicated construction projects with the involvement of multiple parties, fall into delay. When this occurs, the contractor and the employer will almost invariably have different perceptions of the root cause of any such delay and of the responsible party.

More 'formal' contracts (such as the *JCT Standard Form*) have express mechanisms for extending the contractual completion date and for compensating the employer in the form of liquidated damages should the works overrun.

When a project runs into delay, the contractor will often look to the employer for an award of extra time, achieved by extending the completion date for the works. In projects regulated by a standard form contract, it will normally fall to a contractor to apply to the architect or contract administrator for such relief, and the architect or contract administrator will then be charged with deciding whether or the contractor is entitled to be compensated. The contract will frequently oblige the contractor to provide details of any anticipated delay in the form of a notice.

Often compliance with an extension of time provision will not be straightforward. It may require the undertaking of certain technical or administrative obligations in order to substantiate the contractor's claim for extra time and to satisfy the architect, employer or contract administrator that the relief is due. In the course of a busy building project, this may be more than an annoyance for a contractor under pressure to complete; in some circumstances it may be downright onerous. The disgruntled contractor will argue that a failure to serve a timeous notice should not disentitle an award of an extension of time. On the other hand, the employer will argue that contractual provisions requiring a contractor to give notice of delay serve a useful practical purpose and should be adhered to strictly.

It often transpires, upon closer analysis, that alleged causes of delay turn out not to be causes of delay at all, or at least not causes of critical delay. Various factors may combine to cause delay, some of which being the fault of the employer (such as prevention of access to site), some the fault of the contractor (such as insufficient or inefficient labour), and some beyond the control of either party (such as the weather). In such circumstances, a contractor may find it practically impossible to prove that specific events caused particular delays, and is forced to present a claim for an extension of time in a 'global' manner.

This chapter seeks to identify the changing judicial approaches to claims for extensions of time and liquidated damages, and to evaluate the current attitude of the courts towards problematic delay (such as concurrent delay) and 'global' delay claims through a summary of the relevant case law. However, matters such as delay and extensions of time can themselves only be considered if and to the extent that the works in question are to be completed within a certain period of time. Establishing such an obligation is not always straightforward, especially if no express completion date is agreed upon. It is therefore necessary to review the law in this area prior to turning to the matters outlined above in more detail.

4.2 'TIME FOR COMPLETION'

Many building contracts (even the simplest ones) will contain an express provision requiring completion of the works by a certain date. Alternatively, the contract may contain a basic mechanism for computing a completion date, such as a provision obliging a contractor to complete works '24 weeks from commencement on site'. In such cases, it will be incumbent on the contractor to plan his works carefully so as to meet that date, or he will, in principle, be liable to the employer in damages for any delay for which he is responsible.

Some contracts, however, may not have a formal completion date at all. There may be many reasons for this: works may be carried out 'subject to contract' but the contract is never agreed or executed; works may commence pursuant to a letter of intent which contains no completion date; or the parties may simply forget to fill in the appropriate section of a standard form.

Simply because the contract contains no completion date does not mean that the contractor can disregard time as an important factor in his construction programme. If there is no specific time for the completion of the works, then a reasonable time for their completion will be implied. This requirement is now enshrined in statute, but as the following cases demonstrate, it is also a longstanding obligation at common law.

Supply of Goods and Services Act 1982, s. 14

'(1) Where, under a contract for the supply of a service by a supplier acting in the course of business, the time for the service to be carried out is not fixed by the contract, left to be fixed in a manner agreed by the contract or determined by the course of dealing between the parties, there is an implied term that the supplier will carry out the service within a reasonable time.

(2) What is a reasonable time is a question of fact.'

Hick v Raymond & Reid (1893)

This dispute concerned the shipment of a cargo of grain to London under bills of lading which contained no date for when the consignees were to take discharge of the grain. Such discharge was in fact delayed by a dockers' strike. In finding that the consignees were not liable to the shipowner for delay, the House of Lords confirmed that in the absence of a specified date in the contract, the time for performance is within a reasonable time. Lord Herschell L.C. elaborated on this position as follows:

'The only sound principle is that the "reasonable time" should depend upon the circumstances which actually exist ... when I say the circumstances which actually exist,

I of course imply that those circumstances, insofar as they involve delay, have not been caused or contributed to by the consignee.'

Charles Rickards Ltd v Oppenheim (1950)

This case is considered further below in relation to contracts where time is of the essence. In delivering the judgment of the Court of Appeal, Denning LJ considered what was meant by a reasonable time and appeared to approve the submissions made by the appellant:

> 'He cited the well-known words of Lord Watson in *Hick v Raymond and Reid*, that where the law implies that a contract shall be performed within a reasonable time, it had "invariably been held to mean that the party upon whom it is incumbent duly fulfils his obligation, notwithstanding protracted delay, so long as such delay is attributable to causes beyond his control and he has neither acted negligently nor unreasonably."'

Charnock v Liverpool Corp (1968)

The concept of 'reasonable time' emerged in the context of repairs to a motor vehicle following an accident. The repairs took some eight weeks, whereas a competent mechanic could have carried out the same in five. The owner of the vehicle brought an action against the garage for the cost of car hire for the extended repair period of three weeks. The Court of Appeal held that five weeks was a reasonable time for repair, and permitted the relief sought.

British Steel Corp v Cleveland Bridge & Engineering (1981)

This dispute arose out of the manufacture and supply of steel castings required for the formation of the roof nodes at Sama Bank in Damann, Saudi Arabia, pursuant to a letter of intent. At the time, the official form of subcontract had not yet been issued to the claimant manufacturers, but the defendants requested that preparatory works should proceed 'immediately' in any event. The letter of intent contained no delivery date. Procurement and manufacture of the steel was affected by industrial action and various changes to the specification. The claimants sued for the cost of manufacturing the steel. The defendants alleged that the steel was delivered late and out of sequence and counterclaimed accordingly. Whilst the Court concluded that no binding contract was entered into between the parties, Robert Goff J went on to consider the 'reasonableness of the time for performance' in the event that the claimants had been under a duty to complete the works and effect delivery of the steel within a reasonable time. The Court followed the reasoning in *Hick v Raymond & Reid*, and envisaged a two-stage test, as Robert Goff J put it:

> 'As I understand it, I have first to consider what would, in ordinary circumstances, be a reasonable time for the performance of the relevant services [i.e. the manufacture and delivery of the nodes to the required specification]; and I have then to consider to what extent the time for performance by BSC was in fact extended by extraordinary circumstances outside their control.'

In other words, it is clearly not sufficient to look to the 'ordinary time' for the performance of works without regard to the circumstances at the time of performance.

GLC v Cleveland Bridge & Engineering (1984)

The defendants were engaged by the claimant to manufacture, deliver and install steel gates and gate arms for the construction of the Thames Barrier in London. The contract contained various milestone dates by which the defendants were to complete certain phases of the works. The claimant sought to argue that the defendants were under an additional obligation (in the form of an implied term) to proceed with the works generally with due diligence and expedition. The Court of Appeal held that the implication of such a term was not required to give business efficacy to the contract: rather, the defendants were under a duty only to proceed with the diligence that was required to satisfactorily meet the milestone dates and ultimate completion date of the works.

Shawton Engineering v DGP International Ltd (2006)

This recent decision of the Court of Appeal concerned the carrying out of various works in relation to the construction of a process plant for handling nuclear waste at Sellafield. Variations were ordered both before and after the contractual completion date for the works. The contract did not contain any provision for extending time in the event that variations were ordered. The Court of Appeal held that in such circumstances, the effect of the variations was to oblige the contractor to complete the works within a reasonable time, with such reasonableness being judged 'at the time when the question arises in the light of all relevant circumstances'. Whilst not deciding the matter, the Court of Appeal did however cast doubt on the trial judge's conclusions that a 'reasonable time in all the circumstances' would be influenced by the defaulting parties' misapprehension as to the extent of the workscope, and that the effect of instructing a variation was to allow the contractor a reasonable time from the moment for the whole of the remaining work.

Summary

- In the absence of a formal completion date, a reasonable time for completion will normally be implied into a building contract.
- What is a reasonable time for completion will be a matter of fact, to be assessed objectively, at the time when the question arises, according to the circumstances existing at the time of performance.

4.3 ESTABLISHING AN ENTITLEMENT TO AN EXTENSION OF TIME

Many contracts (including standard form contracts, some of which are discussed below) contain express provisions for extending time for completion. In general terms, a contractor must apply for an extension of time and ground his entitlement against a specific contractual provision (known in the JCT forms as 'relevant events'). Such events will broadly cover delay caused by the employer or which is otherwise outwith the contractor's control (such as inclement weather or industrial action).

Often it will be a requirement for the contractor to serve notice on the employer or contract administrator to inform of a particular event which has caused or threatens to cause delay to the works. Sometimes this notice will have to be served in a particular form, by a particular time or be supported by full particulars of the effect of the delay, both in terms of time and money. There really is no substitute for studying the contract carefully: sometimes the service of such notices will be a precondition to relief in the form of an extension of time, and the failure to comply with such contractual mechanisms may be drastic, such as disentitling the contractor from claiming any such extension.

The cases selected below provide some examples of how various issues surrounding extension of time clauses have been dealt with by the courts. In analysing such cases, the courts often have recourse to the 'prevention principle', a rule of law that dictates that no party may insist upon the performance of a particular contractual obligation when that party has prevented such performance from occurring. In the context of building projects and delay, the principle is often extended to prohibit an employer from holding a contractor to a specified completion date in circumstances where an employer act or omission has rendered completion of works by that date impossible. It is precisely to avoid triggering the 'prevention principle' that more sophisticated contracts (including standard forms) contain express mechanisms for extending time. Nevertheless, even in the context of such contracts, disputes concerning the application of the 'prevention principle' still occur, as can be seen from the cases discussed below.

The cases demonstrate that the extension of time mechanism is therefore as much for the benefit of the employer as for the contractor. Without the mechanism, the 'prevention principle' will deprive the employer of the right to levy liquidated damages. Whilst a claim for general damages for delay would then be available, the employer will have to prove its loss.

Holme v Guppy (1838)

The claimants were builders who were engaged by the defendants to carry out various items of carpentry work at a brewery in Liverpool. The contract contained a completion date which gave the claimants four and half months to complete the works following its execution. Delays occurred and various payments were withheld by the defendants, who relied on the fact that the express completion date under the contract had been surpassed, and sought to recover liquidated damages. It transpired that both the claimants and the defendants were culpable for the delay, of which some four weeks was attributable to the defendants' failure to provide access to the site. The Court of the Exchequer considered that this prevention of access was critical, holding that

> 'if the party be prevented by the refusal of the other contracting party from completing the contract within the time limited he is not liable in law for the default...the plaintiffs were therefore left at large. Consequently they are not to forfeit anything for the delay.'

Dodd v Churton (1897)

The claimant builders contended that completion of building works by the contractual completion date had been frustrated by the ordering of additional works by the architect – a common complaint of nineteenth-century and modern-day contractors alike. The Court of Appeal held that whilst the building owner was entitled to compel the contractor to carry out extra works pursuant to a variations clause, that builder could not be held liable for default when he had been prevented from performing his obligations by the acts of the building owner. Lord Esher MR elucidated that 'the reason for that rule is that otherwise a most unreasonable burden would be imposed upon the Contractor.'

Amalgamated Building Contractors Ltd v Waltham Holy Cross UDC (1952)

The claimants were engaged to construct houses pursuant to a standard form of contract issued by RIBA and the National Federation of Building Trades Employers. Building works fell into substantial delay, largely as a result of the contractors' difficulty in procuring labour and materials, which was a contractual ground for an extension of time, which was duly applied for.

The architect did not consider the contractor's claim until after completion of the building works. The contractors claimed that the architect's contractual power to make a 'fair and reasonable extension of time for completion of the works' meant that the architect must exercise this discretion timeously, i.e. so as to give the contractors a date at which they could aim at to complete the works. In other words, the contractors claimed that the power to issue an extension of time could not be exercised retrospectively.

Lord Justice Denning (as he then was) rejected this contention, holding that there was nothing wrong in awarding a retrospective extension of time. It was always open to the contractor to seek relief through arbitration if it was dissatisfied at the architect's dilatory conduct in considering a claim for an extension of time and/or issuing a certificate.

Nowadays, of course, adjudication could provide a swifter resolution.

London Borough of Merton v Stanley Hugh Leach Ltd (1985)

This famous case concerned the construction of some 287 dwellings by the defendant contractor under the *JCT Standard Form of Building Contract, 1963 edition (1971 reissue)* (changes were made to the 1963 form in the 1980 edition). The contract contained the following clause 23:

> 'Upon it becoming reasonably apparent that the progress of the Works is delayed, the Contractor shall forthwith give written notice of the delay to the Architect/Supervising Officer, and if in the opinion of the Architect/Supervising Officer the completion of the works is likely to be or has been delayed beyond the Date for Completion stated in the appendix to these Conditions or beyond any extended time previously fixed under either this clause or clause 33(1)(c) of these Conditions, then the Architect/Supervising Officer shall so soon as he is able to estimate the length of the delay beyond the date or time aforesaid and make in writing a fair and reasonable extension of time for completion of the Works...'

Construction works were indeed delayed, and the contractor contended that such delays were attributable to a lack of cooperation from the claimant borough's architect.

Clause 23 from the JCT Standard Form of Building Contract, 1963 edition (1971 reissue) by the Joint Contracts Tribunal Limited, Sweet & Maxwell, © The Joint Contracts Tribunal Limited, is reproduced here with permission.

The Court made a number of findings which still represent good law in relation to modern day construction disputes where the contract is materially similar. Insofar as it is relevant to extensions of time, the following conclusions were drawn:

- A contractor need not give notice of delay which might be caused by an anticipated future event; rather the contractor's obligations extend to informing the employer of inevitable delay caused by an event which has in fact occurred.
- The giving of notice under clause 23 is not a condition precedent to the architect's consideration of the contractor's entitlement to an extension of time.
- A failure to provide timely notices when the contractor became aware of delay to the progress of the works amounted to a breach of clause 23 of contract.
- A contractor must not benefit from his breach by receiving a greater extension than he would have received had the architect upon notice at the proper time been able to avoid or reduce the delay by some instructions or reasonable requirement.

Peak Construction Ltd v McKinney Foundations Ltd (1970)

Pursuant to a bespoke contract devised by Liverpool Corporation, the claimant builders were engaged to construct a multi-storey block of flats within 24 months. Clause 23 of the contract empowered the architect to extend time in the event of (amongst other things) 'unforeseen circumstances'. The defendants were nominated subcontractors specialising in the design and construction of piles. During the course of the works it was discovered that one of the piles was constructed from unsuitable materials and was, as Salmon LJ put it, 'useless'. Works were immediately suspended and did not recommence for some 58 weeks, ostensibly because the Corporation took its time in deciding upon the most appropriate course of action. Remedial works were eventually carried out which took approximately six weeks to complete.

The Court of Appeal held that it was impossible to hold the contractor responsible for a delay of 58 weeks when the requisite remedial works took only six weeks to complete. In setting out what has become the 'traditional' approach of the courts to the consideration of extension of time and liquidated damages clauses (as to which see below), the Court of Appeal held that the same should be construed strictly *contra proferentem*, and that no liquidated damages would be recoverable where the employer was in any way responsible for a failure to achieve a completion date. Further, their Lordships ruled that if any employer wants to preserve the right to claim liquidated damages in circumstances where he has been culpable for delay, then the extension of time clause should make provision for this eventuality. If this is not catered for in the extension of time clause, then the fixed date for completion will be discharged.

Trolloppe & Colls Ltd v North West Metropolitan Regional Hospital Board (1973)

In this judgment, the House of Lords approved the judgment of Lord Denning MR, sitting in the Court of Appeal, who said that:

> 'It is well settled that in building contracts...when there is stipulation for work to be done in a limited time, if one party by his conduct – it may be quite legitimate conduct, such as ordering extra work – renders it impossible or impracticable for the other party to do his work within the stipulated time, then the one whose conduct caused the trouble can no longer insist upon strict adherence to the time stated. He cannot claim any penalties or liquidated damages for non-completion in that time.'

Bilton v Greater London Council (1982)

In this case, the House of Lords held that the withdrawal of a nominated subcontractor was not the 'fault' of the employer and, in the absence of a contractual provision entitling the contractor to an extension of time therefore, the contractor was not permitted to claim an extension to the completion date. This case is often cited as authority for the proposition that if a contract contains no express power to extend time for a delay which is not the fault of the employer, the contractor assumes risk for that delay.

Bramall & Ogden Ltd v Sheffield City Council (1983)

The claimants were building contractors engaged by the defendant council to carry out various construction works including the erection of a large number of dwellings. Extensions of time were granted to the claimants during the course of the works up to 4 May 1977. The defendant withheld liquidated damages in respect of dwellings which were completed after 4 May 1977. The extension of time clause in question did not cater for the employer's failure to give possession of the whole of the site to the contractor: in the circumstances, the fixed date for completion was discharged and no liquidated damages were recoverable. The Court affirmed the contractual provisions concerning extensions of time and liquidated damages should be construed strictly against an employer.

Walter Lawrence v Commercial Union Properties (1984)

This case concerned the *1963 JCT Standard Form* of contract and the contractor's claim under the same for an extension of time as a result of 'exceptionally inclement weather'.

HHJ Hawser QC held that the effect of the 'exceptionally inclement weather' on the progress of the works is to be assessed at the time when the works are actually carried out, not when they were supposed to be carried out under the construction programme. In other words, when considering a claim for an extension of time arising out of bad weather, the contract administrator (in this case the architect) was not entitled to dismiss the claim simply by stating that the affected works should have been carried out earlier.

Whilst the test is different in related clauses in the 1998 and 2005 JCT Contracts (i.e. 'adverse' rather than 'exceptionally inclement' weather), the principles established in the case as to the relevant period should be of equal effect under these later Forms.

Balfour Beatty Ltd v Chestermount Properties Ltd (1993)

Under the extension of time provisions in the *JCT Standard Form (1980 edition)* the architect had power to grant an extension of time in respect of variations ordered during a period where the contractor was already in culpable delay. Such variations did not therefore constitute acts of prevention setting time at large.

The effect of such variations (and therefore the extension of time) should be considered as the extent to which the period of contract time available for completion ought to be extended or reduced having regard to the incidence of the variations (or other relevant events) (the 'net' approach). The architect was not therefore to assess the length of time required to carry out the variation works and refix the completion date at the end of such period starting from the date of the variation instruction (the 'gross' approach).

John Barker Ltd v London Portman Hotels Ltd (1996)

This dispute concerned refurbishment works to a London hotel under the *JCT Standard Form of Contract (1980 edition)*. The contract provided for sectional completion dates for portions of the work, on a floor-by-floor basis. The parties fell out over the contractor's entitlement for an extension of time which, under the contract, fell to the architect to determine fairly and reasonably.

The Court held that in deliberating over the award of an extension of time, the architect was under an implied obligation to act lawfully, rationally and fairly. This would involve carrying out a logical analysis in a methodical way of the impact that the relevant matters would have on the claimant's construction programme. Further, should the parties be conducting their affairs under a standard form contract with quantities, the architect should pay close attention to the content of the bills before arriving at his decision. It is not necessary to prove bad faith on the part of the architect.

If an extension of time decision is held to be invalid, then the matter might be put back before the architect in question to redetermine the relevant facts and make a fresh award. However, on the facts of the case this was not practically possible, given the absence of contemporaneous notes and the passage of time, as well as undesirable from a costs perspective. In order to get around this problem, the Court ruled that the underlying contractual machinery had broken down to such an extent that the Court could step in to determine what was a fair and reasonable extension of time. The Court hinted that if, on the facts, an architect's award was only invalid in a 'discrete' respect, the matter could be referred afresh for a revised determination.

Turner Corporation Ltd (Receiver and Manager Appointed) v Austotel Pty Ltd (1997)

This case of the Australian courts appears to endorse the movement away from the 'traditional' strict construction of extension of time clauses against an employer in circumstances where a contractor has failed to avail himself of the extension of time mechanism:

> 'If the Builder, having a right to claim an extension of time fails to do so, it cannot claim that the act of prevention which would have entitled it to an extension of time for Practical Completion resulted in its inability to complete by that time. A party to a contract cannot rely upon preventing the contract of the other party where it failed to exercise a contractual right which would have negated the effect of that preventing conduct.'

Gaymark Investments Pty Ltd v Walter Construction Group Ltd (1999)

This case from the Supreme Court of the Northern Territory of Australia concerned a dispute arising out of the construction of a hotel in Darwin. The contract in question (which was based on an Australian standard form) stipulated that the contractor would only be entitled to an extension of time if it had complied strictly with the provisions of the contract imposing conditions on the form, timing and service of notices of delay. In fact, the employer had deleted a provision from the relevant Australian standard form, which entitled the contract administrator to extend time for practical completion even if the appropriate notice had not been served by the contractor.

The works fell behind schedule, eventually amounting to a delay of some 77 days caused by events for which the employer was solely responsible. At arbitration, it was held that notwithstanding the fact that the contractor had failed to comply with the notice provisions of the contract, the 77 days' delay constituted an act of prevention, with the result that there was no date for practical completion and time was put at large.

The Supreme Court agreed, relying on the *contra proferentem* interpretation of extension of time clauses as expressed by Salmon LJ in *Peak v McKinney*, and refused to allow the employer to recover what was described as 'an entirely unmeritorious award of liquidated damages for delays of its own making'.

Sindall Ltd v Solland (2001)

The defendant developer engaged the claimant contractors pursuant to *JCT IFC 1984* terms and conditions to renovate a property known as Lombard House, in Mayfair, London. The works did not run smoothly; following an award of an extension of time (which was later extended following adjudication proceedings), the contract administrator purported to terminate the claimant's employment pursuant to clause 7.2.1 of the contract on the grounds that it was not proceeding diligently with the works. The claimant contractors commenced adjudication proceedings for a declaration that the termination was unlawful, and for an award of a further extension of time.

In enforcing the adjudicator's award, the Court held that when evaluating a claim for an extension of time, a contract administrator should consider all matters which might give rise to a valid claim, not solely those identified and put forward by the contractor. Such considerations would be all the more important where the employer is seeking to determine the contractor's employment by relying on an alleged failure to proceed diligently with the works.

Peninsula Balmain Pty v Abigroup Contractors Ltd (2002)

The defendants in this Australian case in the New South Wales Court of Appeal were contractors engaged to convert former industrial premises into flats. Practical completion was extended by the superintendent (contract administrator) to 26 April 1999; no other extension was sought or grounded. The contract was terminated in December 1999.

The extension of time provision of the contract required the contractor, upon becoming aware of a delay event, to promptly notify the superintendent in writing of the same, and in so doing to include details of the cause and duration of the delay. The Court held that this clause was a condition precedent to the award of an extension of time, and if it was not complied with, the contractor could not rely on the 'prevention' principle to resist a claim for liquidated damages for late completion. Hodgson JA went on, albeit *obiter*, to suggest that a late claim for an extension might fail on the grounds that too much time had elapsed to allow a contract administrator to fairly assess the merits of the same (although this was not the case here).

City Inn Ltd v Shepherd Construction Ltd (2003)

Pursuant to a *JCT Standard Form of Building Contract (1980 edition)*, the claimant employer entered into an agreement with the defendant contractor for the construction of a hotel in Bristol. The contractual completion date passed with the works still unfinished. The contractor blamed the issue of architect's instructions, and was awarded an extension of time of four weeks. Following an adjudication, a further five weeks were granted to the contractor.

The employer contended that the contractor was not entitled to any relief at all and issued proceedings, relying on clause 13.8.5 of the contract which provided that the contractor would not be entitled to an extension of time if it failed to comply with any one or more of the provisions of clause 13.8.1: such provisions required the contractor to identify certain details in writing including initial estimates of loss and expense, the required extension and additional resources, all within 10 days of the delaying event. It was apparently common ground that the contractor had failed to satisfy the requirements of clause 13.8.1.

The Second Division of the Inner House of the Scottish Court of Session sided with the employer, holding that the contractor's failure to comply with the notice requirements was fatal to its claim for an extension of time. The Inner House rejected the contractor's defences that clause 13.8.5 was 'penal'.

In the court below, Lord Macfadyen ruled that the contractor's non-compliance with the special conditions of clause 13.8.1 was a breach of contract, as it deprived the architect of the opportunity to properly reconsider the effect of his notices and to properly consider the extension of time claim. The Second Division of the Inner House did not agree, as clause 13.8.1 did not oblige the contractor to comply with it, but Lord Justice Clerk commented that it was implicit in the contractual arrangement between the parties that the contractor should properly address the likely consequences of any instruction.

It is not clear from the judgment whether the above Australian cases summarised above were cited in argument. Nevertheless, the decision highlights the potential risks to contractors who agree to such notification provisions and fail to comply with them.

McAlpine v Tilebox (2005)

This case is discussed in more detail below: in it, the Court was obliged to consider whether a liquidated damages clause amounted to a penalty. In reaching his judgment, Jackson J appears to suggest that a strict *contra proferentem* approach to the construction of liquidated damages provisions is somewhat outdated, especially given that in most commercial building contracts the employer and contractor operate from positions of equal bargaining power. Although Jackson J's reasoning ultimately relates to a liquidated damages clause, it is suggested that the same can legitimately encompass provisions regarding extensions of time.

Multiplex Constructions (UK) Ltd v Honeywell Control Systems Ltd (No. 2) (2007)

In this recent case of the Technology and Construction Court, Jackson J considered the effect of contractual formalities and preconditions in relation to the award of an extension of time, as well as the application of the 'prevention principle' in such a context. The decision goes some way to resolving what was, at the time, an undecided issue in English law and merits extended analysis.

Honeywell was a specialist subcontractor engaged by Multiplex to design, supply and install various electronic systems at the new national stadium at Wembley. The project was suffering severe delays even prior to Honeywell's commencement of works on site, and delays continued to occur after this time. The parties were at odds over the cause of such delays with Honeywell blaming poor programming and organisation on the part of Multiplex.

Honeywell was directed (pursuant to clause 4.2 of the contract) to comply with three revised programmes issued by Multiplex, each containing progressively later completion dates for the works. The third and final date of 31 March 2006 passed without completion being achieved.

The subcontract between the parties contained the following clause (11.1.3) regarding extensions of time:

> 'It shall be a condition precedent to the Sub-Contractor's [Honeywell's] entitlement to any extension of time under clause 11, that he shall have served all necessary notices on the Contractor [Multiplex] by the dates specified and provided all necessary supporting information including but not limited to causation and effect programmes, labour, plant and materials resource schedules and critical path analysis programmes and the like. In the event the Sub-Contractor fails to notify the Contractor by the dates specified and/or fails to provide any necessary supporting information then he shall waive his right, both under the contract and at common law, in equity and/or pursuant to statute to any entitlement to an extension of time under this clause 11.'

Time for completion and extensions of time

Clause 11.10 contained a list of 'relevant events'. Prior to the litigation, Honeywell had successfully argued in adjudication that Multiplex's directions under clause 4.2 had the effect of putting time at large. Multiplex issued proceedings seeking a declaration that its directions under clause 4.2 did not render time at large. Honeywell's defence included the following grounds:

- As a matter of construction, as a direction under clause 4.2 was not expressly included within the list of relevant events under the extension of time clause and, as a result, Honeywell was unable to claim an extension of time in relation to the same, thus prohibiting Multiplex from insisting on the specified completion date (the 'construction point').
- The extension of time provisions were rendered inoperable by Multiplex, as Multiplex's failure to provide proper programming information rendered compliance with clause 11.1.3 impossible (the 'inoperable point').
- The Court should follow the reasoning of the Australian court in *Gaymark* ('the *Gaymark* point').

Jackson J rejected Honeywell's defences and held that time was not at large: it therefore falls to Honeywell to claim an appropriate extension of time.

As to the 'construction point', Jackson J derived three propositions upon reviewing the relevant authorities:

- actions by the employer which are perfectly legitimate under a construction contract may still be characterised as prevention, if those actions cause delay beyond the contractual completion date;
- acts of prevention by an employer do not set time at large, if the contract provides for extension of time in respect of those events;
- insofar as the extension of time clause is ambiguous, it should be construed in favour of the contractor.

In delivering his judgment, Jackson J followed *Dodd v Churton* and *Trollope v NWMHB* and held that even though directions under clause 4.2 did not automatically qualify for consideration as a 'relevant event' under clause 11.10, they nonetheless fell within clause 11.10 insofar as it provided for 'delay caused by acts of prevention' by Multiplex. Jackson J was not persuaded that a direction causing delay was merely an act of 'hindrance' as opposed to an act of 'prevention'. Such a direction could properly amount to both.

As to the inoperable point, Jackson J held that the wording of the contract obliged Honeywell to do its best as soon as it reasonably could in providing notices or supporting information. Jackson J held that the extension of time provisions were live and properly functioning. It was incumbent on Honeywell to apply for an appropriate extension of time.

As to the '*Gaymark* point', Jackson J stated:

> 'I am bound to say that I see considerable force in the reasoning of the Australian courts in *Turner* and in *Peninsula* and in the reasoning of the Inner House in *City Inn* ... Contractual terms requiring a contractor to give prompt notice of delay serve a valuable purpose; such notice enables matters to be investigated while they are still current. Furthermore, such notice sometimes gives the employer the opportunity to withdraw instructions when the financial consequences become apparent. If *Gaymark* is good law, then a contractor could disregard with impunity any provision making proper notice a condition precedent. At his option the contractor could set time at large.'

In the end, Jackson J did not decide one way or the other, as he distinguished *Gaymark* on the grounds that, unlike in *Gaymark*, the Wembley contract did not automatically expose Honeywell to liquidated damages in the event that the notice clause was not complied with. If Honeywell failed to comply with the provisions, it would be disentitled to an extension of time, but liquidated damages could only be claimed by Multiplex in respect of loss or damage 'caused by the failure of the Sub-Contractor'.

Jackson J also hinted at a movement away from the 'traditional' *contra proferentem* interpretation of extension of time clauses. Although it is unclear from the judgment whether the cases of *McAlpine v Tilebox* and *Murray v Leisureplay* were cited before the Court, Jackson J nonetheless stated that the *contra preferentem* principle should be 'treated with care', indicating that a measured approach is preferable,

Time for completion and extensions of time

as opposed to a blanket application of the doctrine so as to rescue contractors caught by a particular clause:

'... in so far as an extension of time clause is ambiguous, the court should lean in favour of a construction which permits the contractor to recover *appropriate* extensions of time in respect of events causing delay.'

It is suggested that the cogency of Jackson J's judgment and the criticism of commentators such as Professor Ian Duncan Wallace ('Prevention and Liquidated Damages: a theory too far' (2002) 18 *Building and Construction Law*, 82) indicate that it is unlikely that the courts will follow *Gaymark*, except possibly in the most extreme circumstances.

Summary

The following principles can be derived from the various cases summarised above.

- Actions by the employer which are perfectly legitimate under a construction contract may still be characterised as prevention, if those actions cause delay beyond the contractual completion date.
- Acts of prevention by an employer do not set time at large, if the contract provides an extension of time mechanism in respect of those events.
- As modern extension of time clauses often provide for events which have the effect of 'preventing' the contractor from completing works, it is possible that the 'time at large' principle is now less likely to arise in practice.
- A contractor will only be entitled to an extension of time for a delay event which is not the fault of the employer if the contract contains an express provision entitling the contractor in respect of that delay event.
- Delay which is caused by the contractor will not entitle the contractor to an extension of time, unless the contract contains an express term to the contrary (which, it is submitted, would be extraordinary).
- An extension of time may be applied for retrospectively (although in this regard see commentary in relation to the *JCT 2005 form*, set out below).

- If an extension of time clause is subject to preconditions or obliges the contractor to satisfy various requirements, and the contractor fails to do so, the courts will not be afraid of disentitling any award for an extension of time, apparently even if the delay is caused by events for which the employer is responsible. In other words, the 'prevention principle' will not operate so as to trump any requirement for the contractor to comply with preconditions.

- It remains, in theory, possible that a contractor may be able to rely on the reasoning in *Gaymark* (distinguished in *Multiplex v Honeywell*) if a failure to serve notices properly or timeously would open the contractor up to an immediate liability for liquidated damages. However, the tone of the judgment in *Multiplex v Honeywell* suggests that *Gaymark* should be treated with considerable caution.

- Insofar as an extension of time clause is ambiguous, it should be construed in favour of the contractor. However, this should not be overstated so as to provide an escape route for a contractor who has signed up to contract in a position of equal bargaining power to the employer.

- A failure to serve notices timeously or in accordance with the contract may not necessarily amount to a breach: this will depend on the wording of the contract. If it does amount to a breach, it could (in theory) entitle an employer to damages (as to which, see below).

- The employer or contract administrator should act fairly, methodically and logically in considering a claim for an extension of time, and evaluate the impact of each 'event' with regard to the actual progress of works as opposed to the planned progress of works.

- Some clauses may contain clauses which set out which clauses survive termination. An EOT clause will not ordinarily survive termination unless the contract is so worded. See section 5.6.5 below.

4.4 STANDARD FORM CONTRACTS

As set out above, most standard form contracts contain provisions obliging the contractor who claims an extension of time to serve a notice (often within a certain time period)

Time for completion and extensions of time

setting out (at the very least), the length of extension claimed and the reasons for the same. It is then up to the architect, or employer, to grant such an extension as is deemed reasonable.

Delay to a building contract may have serious knock-on effects to the overall construction programme and have substantial ramifications for the critical path of a project. In such circumstances, the architect or contract administrator will want to know as much as possible about the grounds of any such claim in order to ascertain its validity.

4.4.1 JCT 2005

Broadly speaking, under the *JCT* forms of contract, a contractor will be permitted to obtain extension of time when matters outwith his control have the effect of delaying the works. In practical terms, it will fall to the contract administrator, architect or employer's agent, depending on the particular form, to assess how much time (if any) should be allowed. The contractor will nonetheless be obliged to take all reasonable measures to mitigate any such delay. The more sophisticated *JCT* forms provide for an extension of time upon certain specific 'events'. If event in fact causing delay to the contractor is one of the 'events' provided for in the contract, he will be entitled to an extension of time to the completion date, and no liquidated damages will be levied for that period. In short, the extension of time provision is a shorthand recording of how various risks associated with a building contract are to be divided between the contractor and the employer. These provisions are often subject to bespoke amendments. There is no substitute for reading the contract carefully, as the cases selected above demonstrate.

Most of the grounds for an extension of time under *JCT 1998* have been adopted under *JCT 2005*, but the 2005 suite has seen a rationalising of 'relevant events' One notable difference is that non-availability of labour and materials is no longer a relevant event. Without a bespoke amendment, the risk of delay and/or disruption resulting from problems with supply of labour, plant or materials appears to shift to the contractor.

Space does not permit an in-depth analysis of all of the *JCT* provisions in respect of extensions of time, but the relevant terms of some of the contracts in the *JCT 2005* suite are discussed below.

Minor Works (MW/MWD)

'If it becomes apparent that the Works will not be completed by the Date for Completion stated in the Contract Particulars (or any later date fixed in accordance with the provisions of this clause 2.7) for reasons beyond the control of the Contractor, including compliance with any instruction of the Architect/Contract Administrator under this Contract whose issue is not due to a default of the Contractor, then the Contractor shall thereupon in writing so notify the Architect/Contract Administrator who shall make, in writing, such extension of time for completion as may be reasonable. Reasons within the control of the Contractor include any default of the Contractor or of others employed or engaged by or under him for or in connection with the Works and of any supplier of goods or materials for the Works.'

Clauses from the JCT Minor Works Contract (2005 edition) by the Joint Contracts Tribunal Limited, Sweet & Maxwell, © The Joint Contracts Tribunal Limited, are reproduced here with permission.

The award of any extension of time is left to the discretion of the architect/contract administrator provided that the matters in question are outwith the contractor's control.

It is possible that the contractor may be in a more favourable position under MW/MWD than the other *JCT 2005* forms, where an extension of time is contingent upon 'relevant events'. In other words, in the other forms, risk in respect of delay is more specifically allocated between the parties.

Whilst the supply of written notice is a mandatory requirement it is not thought that this will amount to a condition precedent to the granting of an extension of time, as it is not expressly stated to have this effect and there is no indication of what consequence would follow from the failure to provide appropriate written notice.

Intermediate Form (IC/ICD)

'Adjustment of Completion Date

Notice of delay – extensions

Time for completion and extensions of time

2.19 1 If and whenever it becomes reasonably apparent that the progress of the Works or any Section is being or is likely to be delayed the Contractor shall forthwith give written notice of the cause of the delay to the Architect/Contract Administrator, and if in the opinion of the Architect/Contract Administrator the completion of the Works or Section has been, is being or is likely to be delayed beyond the relevant Completion Date by any of the Relevant Events, then, save where these Conditions expressly provide otherwise, the Architect/Contract Administrator shall as soon as he is able to estimate the length of delay beyond that date make in writing a fair and reasonable extension of time for completion of the Works or Section.

2 If any Relevant Event referred to in clauses 2.20.1 to 2.20.6 occurs after the relevant Completion Date but before practical completion is achieved, the Architect/Contract Administrator shall so soon as he is able to estimate the length of the delay, if any, to the Works or any Section resulting from that event make in writing a fair and reasonable extension of the time for completion of the Works or Section.

3 At any time up to 12 weeks after the date of practical completion of the Works or Section, the Architect/ Contract Administrator may make an extension of time in accordance with the provisions of this clause 2.19, whether upon reviewing a previous decision or otherwise and whether or not the Contractor has given notice as referred to in clause 2.19.1 Such an extension of time shall not reduce any previously made.

4 Provided always that the Contractor shall:

> 1 constantly use his best endeavours to prevent delay and shall do all that may reasonably be required to the satisfaction of the Architect/Contract Administrator to proceed with the Works or Section; and

> 2 provide such information required by the Architect/Contract Administrator as is reasonably necessary for the purposes of this clause 2.19.

5 In this clause 2.19 and, so far as relevant, in the other clauses of these Conditions, any reference to delay or extension of time includes any further delay or further extension of time.

Relevant Events

2.20 The following are the Relevant Events referred to in clause 2.19:

1 Variations and any other matters or instructions which under these Conditions are to be treated as, or as requiring, a Variation;

2 instructions of the Architect/Contract Administrator:

> 1 under any of clauses 2.13, 3.12 or 3.13 (excluding, where there are Contract Bills, an instruction for expenditure of a Provisional Sum for defined work);
>
> 2 (to the extent provided therein) under clause 3.7 and Schedule 2; or
>
> 3 for the opening up for inspection or testing of any work, materials or goods under clause 3.14 or 3.15.1 (including making good), unless the inspection or test shows that the work, materials or goods are not in accordance with this Contract;

3 deferment of the giving of possession of the site or any Section under clause 2.5;

4 the execution of work for which an Approximate Quantity is not a reasonably accurate forecast of the quantity of work required;

5 suspension by the Contractor under clause 4.11 of the performance of his obligations under this Contract;

6 any impediment, prevention or default, whether by act or omission, by the Employer, the Architect/Contract Administrator, the Quantity Surveyor or any of the Employer's Persons, except to the extent caused or contributed to by any default, whether by act or omission, of the Contractor or of any of the Contractor's Persons;

Time for completion and extensions of time

7 the carrying out by a Statutory Undertaker of work in pursuance of its statutory obligations in relation to the Works, or the failure to carry out such work;

8 exceptionally adverse weather conditions;

9 loss or damage occasioned by any of the Specified Perils;

10 civil commotion or the use or threat of terrorism and/or the activities of the relevant authorities in dealing with such event or threat;

11 strike, lock-out or local combination of workmen affecting any of the trades employed upon the Works or any of the trades engaged in the preparation, manufacture or transportation of any of the goods or materials required for the Works;

12 the exercise after the Base Date by the United Kingdom Government of any statutory power which directly affects the execution of the Works;

13 force majeure.'

Clauses from the JCT Intermediate Form Contract (2005 edition) by the Joint Contracts Tribunal Limited, Sweet & Maxwell, © The Joint Contracts Tribunal Limited, are reproduced here with permission.

The effect of this clause in the *1963 Standard Form of Building Contract* (which is worded in similar terms to *IC 2005*) has been considered above in *Merton v Leach*.

The wording of *IC 2005* (and of the *JCT Intermediate Form of Building Contract 1998 edition*) suggests that the contractor's service of a notice will not be a condition precedent to the performance by the architect of his duties under the clause.

Standard Building Contract (SBQ)

'Adjustment of Completion Date

Related definitions and interpretation

2.26 In clauses 2.27 to 2.29 and, so far as relevant, in the other clauses of these Conditions:

1 any reference to delay or extension of time includes any further delay or further extension of time;

2 "Pre-agreed Adjustment" means the fixing of a revised Completion Date for the Works or a Section in respect of a Variation or other work referred to in clause 5.2.1 by the Confirmed Acceptance of a Schedule 2 Quotation;

3 "Relevant Omission" means the omission of any work or obligation through an instruction for a Variation under clause 3.14 or through an instruction under clause 3.16 in regard to a Provisional Sum for defined work.

Notice by Contractor of delay to progress

2.27 1 If and whenever it becomes reasonably apparent that the progress of the Works or any Section is being or is likely to be delayed the Contractor shall forthwith give written notice to the Architect/Contract Administrator of the material circumstances, including the cause or causes of the delay, and shall identify in the notice any event which in his opinion is a Relevant Event.

2 In respect of each event identified in the notice the Contractor shall, if practicable in such notice or otherwise in writing as soon as possible thereafter, give particulars of its expected effects, including an estimate of any expected delay in the completion of the Works or any Section beyond the relevant Completion Date.

3 The Contractor shall forthwith notify the Architect/Contract Administrator in writing of any material change in the estimated delay or in any other particulars and supply such further information as the Architect/Contract Administrator may at any time reasonably require.

Fixing Completion Date

2.28 1 If, in the opinion of the Architect/Contract Administrator, on receiving a notice and particulars under clause 2.27:

1 any of the events which are stated to be a cause of delay is a Relevant Event; and

2 completion of the Works or of any Section is likely to be delayed thereby beyond the relevant Completion Date,

Time for completion and extensions of time

then, save where these Conditions expressly provide otherwise, the Architect/Contract Administrator shall give an extension of time by fixing such later date as the Completion Date for the Works or Section as he then estimates to be fair and reasonable,

2 Whether or not an extension is given, the Architect/Contract Administrator shall notify the Contractor in writing of his decision in respect of any notice under clause 2.27 as soon as is reasonably practicable and in any event within 12 weeks of receipt of the required particulars. Where the period from receipt to the Completion Date is less than 12 weeks, he shall endeavour to do so prior to the Completion Date.

3 The Architect/Contract Administrator shall in his decision state:

> 1 the extension of time that he has attributed to each Relevant Event; and
>
> 2 (in the case of a decision under clause 2.28.4 or 2.28.5) the reduction in time that he has attributed to each Relevant Omission.

4 After the first fixing of a later Completion Date in respect of the Works or a Section, either under clause 2.28.1 or by a Pre-agreed Adjustment, but subject to clauses 2.28.6.3 and 2.28.6.4, the Architect/Contract Administrator may by notice in writing to the Contractor, giving the details referred to in clause 2.28.3, fix a Completion Date for the Works or that Section earlier than that previously so fixed if in his opinion the fixing of such earlier Completion Date is fair and reasonable, having regard to any Relevant Omissions for which instructions have been issued after the last occasion on which a new Completion Date was fixed for the Works or for that Section.

5 After the Completion Date for the Works or for a Section, if this occurs before the date of practical completion, the Architect/Contract Administrator may, and not later than the expiry of 12 weeks after the date of practical completion shall, by notice in writing to the Contractor, giving the details referred to in clause 2.28.3:

> > 1 fix a Completion Date for the Works or for the Section later than that previously fixed if in his opinion that is fair and reasonable having regard to any Relevant Events, whether on reviewing a previous decision or otherwise and whether or not the Relevant Event has been specifically notified by the Contractor under clause 2.27.1; or
>
> > 2 subject to clauses 2.28.6.3 and 2.28.6.4, fix a Completion Date earlier than that previously fixed if in his opinion that is fair and reasonable having regard to any instructions for Relevant Omissions issued after the last occasion on which a new Completion Date was fixed for the Works or Section; or
>
> > 3 confirm the Completion Date previously fixed.
>
> 6 Provided always that:
>
> > 1 the Contractor shall constantly uses his best endeavours to prevent delay in the progress of the Works or any Section, however caused, and to prevent the completion of the Works or Section being delayed or further delayed beyond the relevant Completion Date;
>
> > 2 in the event of any delay the Contractor shall do all that may reasonably be required to the satisfaction of the Architect/Contract Administrator to proceed with the Works or Section;
>
> > 3 no decision of the Architect/Contract Administrator under clause 2.28.4 or 2.28.5.2 shall fix a Completion Date for the Works or any Section earlier than the relevant Date for Completion; and
>
> > 4 no decision under clause 2.28.4 or 2.28.5.2 shall alter the length of any Pre-agreed Adjustment unless the relevant Variation or other work referred to in clause 521 is itself the subject of a Relevant Omission.
>
> **Relevant Events**
>
> 2.29 The following are the Relevant Events referred to in clauses 2.27 and 2.28:

Time for completion and extensions of time

1 Variations and any other matters or instructions which under these Conditions are to be treated as, or as requiring, a Variation;

2 instructions of the Architect/Contract Administrator:

> 1 under any of clauses 2.15, 3.15, 31.6 (excluding an instruction for expenditure of a Provisional Sum for defined work), 3.23 or 5.3.2; or
>
> 2 for the opening up for inspection or testing of any work, materials or goods under clause 3.17 or 3.18.4 (including making good), unless the inspection or test shows that the work, materials or goods are not in accordance with this Contract;

3 deferment of the giving of possession of the site or any Section under clause 2.5;

4 the execution of work for which an Approximate Quantity is not a reasonably accurate forecast of the quantity of work required;

5 suspension by the Contractor under clause 4.14 of the performance of his obligations under this Contract;

6 any impediment, prevention or default, whether by act or omission, by the Employer, the Architect/Contract Administrator, the Quantity Surveyor or any of the Employer's Persons, except to the extent caused or contributed to by any default, whether by act or omission, of the Contractor or of any of the Contractor's Persons;

7 the carrying out by a Statutory Undertaker of work in pursuance of its statutory obligations in relation to the Works, or the failure to carry out such work;

8 exceptionally adverse weather conditions;

9 loss or damage occasioned by any of the Specified Perils;

10 civil commotion or the use or threat of terrorism and/or the activities of the relevant authorities In dealing with such event or threat;

11 strike, lock-out or local combination of workmen affecting any of the trades employed upon the Works or any of the trades engaged in the preparation, manufacture or

transportation of any of the goods or materials required for the Works or any persons engaged in the preparation of the design for the Contractor's Designed Portion;

12 the exercise after the Base Date by the United Kingdom Government of any statutory power which directly affects the execution of the Works;

13 force majeure.'

Clauses from the JCT Standard Building Contract (2005 edition) by the Joint Contracts Tribunal Limited, Sweet & Maxwell, © The Joint Contracts Tribunal Limited, are reproduced here with permission.

The effect of this clause in the *1963 Standard Form of Building Contract* (which is worded in similar terms to *IC 2005*) has been considered above in *Merton v Leach*. In that case, it was held that the giving of written notice was not a condition precedent to the performance by the architect of his duties under the clause. However, failure by the contractor to give notice was a breach of contract and this breach could be taken into account by the architect in making the extension of time.

It is thought that such a notice may well be a condition precedent to the grant of an extension *prior* to practical completion. However, a notice is not a precondition to claiming an extension of time after practical completion, as the employer is obliged under clause 2.28.5 to consider all relevant events whether or not they have been previously communicated to the employer. (See e.g. the views of the editors of *Keating on JCT Contracts* at 1.1–103.)

In practical terms, the contractor's failure to supply a contemporaneous notice may cast evidential doubt over the validity of an application for an extension of time after practical completion. The employer will argue that if the delay event was so serious, the contractor could at least have notified him of the same. However, as set out above in *Merton v Leach*, by not supplying a notice, the contractor will be in breach of contract, and it is suggested that he will not be entitled to a more generous extension when he applies after practical completion than he would have received at the time of the delaying event that he later relies upon. Timeous serving of notices empowers the architect or contract administrator to

Time for completion and extensions of time

avoid or reduce any delay by issuing appropriate instructions: damages may flow from this breach if it can be established that the employer lost an opportunity to mitigate delay or disruption for which, in principle, the contractor is entitled to relief.

The *JCT 2005* standard form of contract refers to 'adverse weather conditions' as opposed to 'exceptionally inclement weather'. It is thought that this does not amount to any material difference.

Design and Build Contract (DB)

'Adjustment of Completion Date

Related definitions and interpretation

2.23 In clauses 2.24 to 2.26 and, so far as relevant, in the other clauses of these Conditions:

1 any reference to delay or extension of time includes any further delay or further extension of time;

2 "Pre-agreed Adjustment" means the fixing of a revised Completion tale for the Works or a Section in respect of a Change or other work referred to in clause 5.2;

3 "Relevant Omission" means the omission of any work obligation through an instruction for a Change under clause 39.

Notice by Contractor of delay to progress

2.24 1 If and whenever it becomes reasonably apparent that the progress of the Works or any Section is being or is likely to be delayed the Contractor shall forthwith give written notice to the Employer of the material circumstances, including the cause or causes of the delay, and shall identify in the notice any event which in his opinion is a Relevant Event.

2 In respect of each event identified in the notice the Contractor shall, if practicable in such notice or otherwise in writing as soon as possible thereafter, give particulars of its expected effects, including an estimate of any expected delay in the completion of the Works or any Section beyond the relevant Completion Date.

93

3 The Contractor shall forthwith notify the Employer in writing of any material change in the estimated delay or In any other particulars and supply such further information as the Employer may at any time reasonably require.

Fixing Completion Date

2.25 1 If on receiving a notice and particulars under clause 2.24:

> 1 any of the events which are stated to be a cause of delay is a Relevant Event; and
>
> 2 completion of the Works or of any Section is likely to be delayed thereby beyond the relevant Completion Date,

then, save where these Conditions expressly provide otherwise, the Employer shall give an extension of time by fixing such later date as the Completion Date for the Works or Section as he then estimates to be fair and reasonable.

2 Whether or not an extension is given, the Employer shall notify the Contractor in writing of his decision in respect of any notice under clause 2.24 as soon as is reasonably practicable and in any event within 12 weeks of receipt of the required particulars. Where the period from receipt to the Completion Date is less than 12 weeks, he shall endeavour to do so prior to the Completion Date.

3 The Employer shall in his decision state:

> 1 the extension of time that he has attributed to each Relevant Event; and
>
> 2 (in the case of a decision under clause 2.25.4 or 2.25.5) the reduction in time that he has attributed to each Relevant Omission.

4 After the first fixing of a later Completion Date in respect of the Works or a Section, either under clause 2.25.1 or by a Pre-agreed Adjustment, but subject to clauses 2.25.6.3 and 2.25.6.4, the Employer may by notice in writing to the Contractor, giving the details referred to in clause 2.25.3, fix a Completion Date for the Works or that Section earlier than that previously so fixed if the fixing of such earlier Completion Date is fair and reasonable, having regard to

Time for completion and extensions of time

any Relevant Omissions for which Instructions have been issued after the last occasion on which a new Completion Date was fixed for the Works or for that Section.

5 After the Completion Date for the Works or for a Section, if this occurs before the date of practical completion, the Employer may, and not later than the expiry of 12 weeks after the date of practical completion shall, by notice in writing to the Contractor, giving the details referred to in clause 2.25.3:

> 1 fix a Completion Date for the Works or for the Section later than that previously fixed if it is fair and reasonable having regard to any Relevant Events whether on reviewing a previous decision or otherwise and whether or not the Relevant Event has been specifically notified by the Contractor under clause 2.24.1; or

> 2 subject to clauses 2.25.6.3 and 2.25.6.4 fix a Completion Date earlier than that previously fixed if that is fair and reasonable having regard to any instructions for Relevant Omissions issued after the last occasion on which a new Completion Date was fixed for the Works or Section; or

> 3 confirm the Completion Date previously fixed.

6 Provided always that:

> 1 the Contractor Shall constantly use his best endeavours to prevent delay in the progress of the Works or any Section, however caused, and to prevent the completion of the Works or Section being delayed or further delayed beyond the relevant Completion Date;

> 2 in the event of any delay the Contractor shall do all that may reasonably be required to the satisfaction of the Employer to proceed with the Works or Section;

> 3 no decision of the Employer under clause 2.25.4 or 2.25.5.2 shall fix a Completion Date for the Works or any Section earlier than the relevant Date for Completion; and

4 no decision under clause 2.25.4 or 2.25.5.2 shall alter the length of any Pre-agreed Adjustment unless the relevant Change or other work referred to in clause 52 is itself the subject of a Relevant Omission.

Relevant Events

2.26 The following are the Relevant Events referred to in clauses 2.24 and 2.25:

1 Changes and any other matters or instructions which under these Conditions are to be treated as, or as requiring, a Change;

2 instructions of the Employer:

> 1 under any of clauses 2.13, 3.10, 3.11 or 3.16; or
>
> 2 for the opening up for inspection or testing of any work, materials or goods under clause 3.12 or 3.13.3 (including making good), unless the inspection or test shows that the work, materials or goods are not in accordance with this Contract;

3 deferment of the giving of possession of the site or any Section under clause 2.4;

4 suspension by the Contractor under clause 4.11 of the performance of his obligations under this Contract;

5 any impediment, prevention or default, whether by act or omission, by the Employer or any of the Employer's Persons, except to the extent caused or contributed to by any default, whether by act or omission, of the Contractor or of any of the Contractor's Persons;

6 the carrying out by a Statutory Undertaker of work in pursuance of its statutory obligations in relation to the Works, or the failure to carry out such work;

7 exceptionally adverse weather conditions;

8 loss or damage occasioned by any of the Specified Perils;

9 civil commotion or the use or threat of terrorism and/or the activities of the relevant authorities in dealing with such event or threat;

Time for completion and extensions of time

10 strike, lock-out or local combination of workmen affecting any of the trades employed upon the Works or any of the trades engaged in the preparation, manufacture or transportation of any f the goods or materials required for the Works or any persons engaged in the preparation of the design for the Works;

11 the exercise after the Base Date by the United Kingdom Government of any statutory power which directly affects the execution of the Works;

12 delay in receipt of any necessary permission or approval of any statutory body which the Contractor has taken all practicable steps to avoid or reduce,

13 force majeure.'

Clauses from the JCT Design and Build Contract (2005 edition) by the Joint Contracts Tribunal Limited, Sweet & Maxwell, © The Joint Contracts Tribunal Limited, are reproduced here with permission.

The relevant wording to a large extent mirrors the wording of the standard form: refer to the discussion of *SBQ* above.

4.4.2 ICE (7th edition)

'Extension of time for completion

44 (1) Should the Contractor consider that:

(a) any variation ordered under Clause 51(1) or

(b) increased quantities referred to in Clause 51(4) or

(c) any cause of delay referred to in these Conditions or

(d) exceptional adverse weather conditions or

(e) any delay impediment prevention or default by the Employer or

(f) other special circumstances of any kind whatsoever which may occur

be such as to entitle him to an extension of time for the substantial completion of the Works or any Section thereof he shall within 28 days after the cause of any delay has arisen or as soon thereafter as is reasonable deliver to the

Engineer full and detailed particulars in justification of the period of extension claimed in order that the claim may be investigated at the time.

Assessment of delay

(2) (a) The Engineer shall upon receipt of such particulars consider all the circumstances known to him at that time and make an assessment of the delay (if any) that has been suffered by the Contractor as a result of the alleged cause and shall so notify the Contractor in writing.

(b) The Engineer may in the absence of any claim make an assessment of the delay that he considers has been suffered by the Contractor as a result of any of the circumstances listed in sub-clause (1) of this Clause and shall so notify the Contractor in writing.

Interim grant of extension of time

(3) Should the Engineer consider that the delay suffered fairly entitles the Contractor to an extension of the time for the substantial completion of the Works or any Section thereof such interim extension shall be granted forthwith and be notified to the Contractor in writing with a copy to the Employer. In the event that the Contractor has made a claim for an extension of time but the Engineer does not consider the Contractor entitled to an extension of time he shall so inform the Contractor without delay.

Assessment at due date for completion

(4) The Engineer shall not later than 14 days after the due date or extended date for completion of the Works or any Section thereof (and whether or not the Contractor shall have made any claim for an extension of time) consider all the circumstances known to him at that time and take action similar to that provided for in sub-clause (3) of this Clause. Should the Engineer consider that the Contractor is not entitled to an extension of time he shall so notify the Employer and the Contractor.

Final determination of extension

(5) The Engineer shall within 28 days of the issue of the Certificate of Substantial Completion for the Works or for any Section thereof review all the circumstances of the kind

Time for completion and extensions of time

referred to in sub-clause (1) of this Clause and shall finally determine and certify to the Contractor with a copy to the Employer the overall extension of time (if any) to which he considers the Contractor entitled in respect of the Works or the relevant Section. No such final review of the circumstances shall result in a decrease in any extension of time already granted by the Engineer pursuant to sub-clauses (3) or (4) of this Clause.'

Clauses from the ICE Conditions of Contract (7th edition), published by Thomas Telford and the Institution of Civil Engineers, are reproduced with permission.

The 7th edition of the form includes a 'catch-all' provision at clause 44(1)(e) which did not form part of the previous editions of the ICE form. This is to get around the problems of the clause becoming invalidated, and time being put at large, in the event of an employer event which is not catered for in the EOT machinery (as to which, see the cases discussed above).

It is not thought that clause 44(1) is a condition precedent to the recovery of an extension of time: the contractor may deliver his claim 'as soon thereafter as is reasonable.'

4.4.3 NEC3

'60 Compensation events

60.1 The following are compensation events.

(1) The Project Manager gives an instruction changing the Works Information except

- a change made in order to accept a Defect or

- a change to the Works Information provided by the Contractor for his design which is made either at his request or to comply with other Works Information provided by the Employer.

(2) The Employer does not allow access to and use of a part of the Site by the later of its access date and the date shown on the Accepted Programme.

(3) The Employer does not provide something which he is to provide by the date for providing it shown on the Accepted Programme.

(4) The Project Manager gives an instruction to stop or not to start any work or to change a Key Date.

(5) The Employer or Others

- do not work within the times shown on the Accepted Programme,

- do not work within the conditions stated in the Works Information or

- carry out work on the Site that is not stated in the Works Information.

(6) The Project Manager or the Supervisor does not reply to a communication from the Contractor within the period required by this contract.

(7) The Project Manager gives an instruction for dealing with an object of value or of historical or other interest found within the Site.

(8) The Project Manager or the Supervisor changes a decision which he has previously communicated to the Contractor.

(9) The Project Manager withholds an acceptance (other than acceptance of a quotation for acceleration or for not correcting a Defect) for a reason not stated in this contract.

(10) The Supervisor instructs the Contractor to search for a Defect and no Defect is found unless the search is needed only because the Contractor gave insufficient notice of doing work obstructing a required test or inspection.

(11) A test or inspection done by the Supervisor causes unnecessary delay.

(12) The Contractor encounters physical conditions which

- are within the Site,

- are not weather conditions and

- an experienced contractor would have judged at the Contract Date to have such a small chance of occurring that it would have been unreasonable for him to have allowed for them.

Time for completion and extensions of time

Only the difference between the physical conditions encountered and those for which it would have been reasonable to have allowed is taken into account in assessing a compensation event.

(13) A weather measurement is recorded

- within a calendar month,
- before the Completion Date for the whole of the works and
- at the place stated in the Contract Data

the value of which, by comparison with the weather data, is shown to occur on average less frequently than once in ten years.

Only the difference between the weather measurement and the weather which the weather data show to occur on average less frequently than once in ten years is taken into account in assessing a compensation event.

(14) An event which is an Employer's risk stated in this contract.

(15) The Project Manager certifies take over of a part of the works before both Completion and the Completion Date.

(16) The Employer does not provide materials, facilities and samples for tests and inspections as stated in the Works Information.

(17) The Project Manager notifies a correction to an assumption which he has stated about a compensation event.

(18) A breach of contract by the Employer which is not one of the other compensation events in this contract.

(19) An event which

- stops the Contractor completing the works or
- stops the Contractor completing the works by the date shown on the Accepted Programme,

and which

- neither Party could prevent,

- an experienced contractor would have judged at the Contract Date to have such a small chance of occurring that it would have been unreasonable for him to have allowed for it and

is not one of the other compensation events stated in this contract.

60.2 In judging the physical conditions for the purpose of assessing a compensation event, the Contractor is assumed to have taken into account

- the Site Information,

- publicly available information referred to in the Site Information,

- information obtainable from a visual inspection of the Site and

- other information which an experienced contractor could reasonably be expected to have or to obtain.

60.3 If there is an ambiguity or inconsistency within the Site Information (including the information referred to in it), the Contractor is assumed to have taken into account the physical conditions more favourable to doing the work.

61 Notifying Compensation events

61.1 For compensation events which arise from the Project Manager or the Supervisor giving an instruction or changing an earlier decision, the Project Manager notifies the Contractor of the compensation event at the time of giving the instruction or changing the earlier decision. He also instructs the Contractor to submit quotations, unless the event arises from a fault of the Contractor or quotations have already been submitted. The Contractor puts the instruction or changed decision into effect.

61.2 The Project Manager may instruct the Contractor to submit quotations for a proposed instruction or a proposed changed decision The Contractor does not put a proposed instruction or a proposed changed decision into effect.

61.3 The Contractor notifies the Project Manager of an event which has happened or which he expects to happen as a compensation event if

Time for completion and extensions of time

- the Contractor believes that the event is a compensation event and

- the Project Manager has not notified the event to the Contractor If the Contractor does not notify a compensation event within eight weeks of becoming aware of the event, he is not entitled to a change in the Prices the Completion Date or a Key Date unless the Project Manager should have notified the event to the Contractor but did not.

61.4 If the Project Manager decides that an event notified by the Contractor

- arises from a fault of the Contractor,

- has not happened and is not expected to happen,

- has no effect upon Defined Cost, Completion or meeting a Key Date or

- is not one of the compensation events stated in this contract

he notifies the Contractor of his decision that the Prices, the Completion Date and the Key Dates are not to be changed.

If the Project Manager decides otherwise, he notifies the Contractor accordingly and instructs him to submit quotations.

If the Project Manager does not notify his decision to the Contractor within either

- one week of the Contractor's notification or

- a longer period to which the Contractor has agreed,

the Contractor may notify the Project Manager to this effect. A failure by the Project Manager to reply within two weeks of this notification is treated as acceptance by the Project Manager that the event is a compensation event and an instruction to submit quotations.

61.5 If the Project Manager decides that the Contractor did not give an early warning of the event which an experienced contractor could have given, he notifies this decision to the Contractor when he instructs him to submit quotations.

61.6 If the Project Manager decides that the effects of a compensation event are too uncertain to be forecast reasonably, he states assumptions about the event in his instruction to the Contractor to submit quotations. Assessment of the event is based on these assumptions. If any of them is later found to have been wrong, the Project Manager notifies a correction.

61.7 A compensation event is not notified after the defects date.

62 Quotations for compensation events

62.1 After discussing with the Contractor different ways of dealing with the compensation event which are practicable, the Project Manager may instruct the Contractor to submit alternative quotations. The Contractor submits the required quotations to the Project Manager and may submit quotations for other methods of dealing with the compensation event which he considers practicable.

62.2 Quotations for compensation events comprise proposed changes to the Prices and any delay to the Completion Date and Key Dates assessed by the Contractor. The Contractor submits details of his assessment with each quotation. If the programme for remaining work is altered by the compensation event, the Contractor includes the alterations to the Accepted Programme in his quotation.

62.3 The Contractor submits quotations within three weeks of being instructed to do so by the Project Manager. The Project Manager replies within two weeks of the submission. His reply is

- an instruction to submit a revised quotation,

- an acceptance of a quotation,

- a notification that a proposed instruction will not be given or a proposed changed decision will not be made or

- a notification that he will be making his own assessment.

62.4 The Project Manager instructs the Contractor to submit a revised quotation only after explaining his reasons for

Time for completion and extensions of time

doing so to the Contractor. The Contractor submits the revised quotation within three weeks of being instructed to do so.

62.5 The Project Manager extends the time allowed for

- the Contractor to submit quotations for a compensation event and
- the Project Manager to reply to a quotation

if the Project Manager and the Contractor agree to the extension before the submission or reply is due. The Project Manager notifies the extension that has been agreed to the Contractor.

62.6 If the Project Manager does not reply to a quotation within the time allowed, the Contractor may notify the Project Manager to this effect. If the Contractor submitted more than one quotation for the compensation event, he states in his notification which quotation he proposes is to be accepted. If the Project Manager does not reply to the notification within two weeks, and unless the quotation is for a proposed instruction or a proposed changed decision, the Contractor's notification is treated as acceptance of the quotation by the Project Manager.'

Clauses from the NEC3 Engineering and Construction Contract are reproduced here with permission from NEC Contracts.

An extension of time will be awarded to the contractor under the *NEC3* if he can prove that a 'compensation event' (broadly speaking, and event which does not arise from the contractor's fault) will affect the completion date. (The position regarding *NEC3* and the "float" is set out below.) Pursuant to clause 61, either the contractor or the project manager may notify the other or a compensation event.

The process of dealing with 'compensation events' is discursive: the contractor is invited to submit quotations in respect of the requisite works to deal with the same.

However, clause 61.3 contains an important 'time-barring' provision: should the contractor fail to notify a compensation event within eight weeks of becoming aware of that event, he will not recover relief either in the form of time or money, unless the project manager should have notified the contractor of the event but did not.

4.5 DELAY AND DETERMINATION – TIME OF THE ESSENCE

If the contractor is responsible for delay, then this will amount to a breach of contract and the employer will be entitled to damages. However, a particularly disgruntled employer may be keen to eject a contractor from site if the works in question have fallen into delay. This section explores the circumstances in which an employer will be entitled to do so.

Felton v Wharrie (1906)

The claimant was a building contractor who was engaged by the defendant to pull down houses on the defendant's site within 42 working days. The contract provided that liquidated damages would be payable at a daily rate for every day after the completion date that the properties remained on site. The contractor failed to finish the works in the stipulated time, and was duly asked by the employer whether or not the work would be finished within four months. The contractor was unsure, and thus unable to commit to any firm completion date. After two weeks, the employer ejected the contractor from site and engaged a third party contractor to complete the demolition works. The Court of Appeal held that the employer was wrong to do so, stating that:

> 'If he were going to act upon the claimant's conduct as being evidence of his not going on, he ought to have told him of it, and to have said "I treat that as a refusal", and the man would know of it; but the fact of allowing him to go on cannot be any evidence of justification of re-entry.'

Lucas v Godwin (1837)

The claimant bricklayer contracted to carry out various items of stonework and roofwork to six cottages to be erected on the defendant's land, and brought an action to procure payment from the defendant. In delivering its judgment, the Court held that, notwithstanding the existence of a

Time for completion and extensions of time

contractual completion date, completion by such date did not 'go to the essence' of the contract, as the employer could be adequately compensated in damages for any delay.

Rickards v Oppenheim (1950)

This case concerned the delivery of a chassis for a Rolls-Royce motor car. However, the principles set out by the Court of Appeal are relevant to construction disputes. Their Lordships held that absent a contractual stipulation that time is of the essence, an employer may serve a notice making time of the essence of the contract. The reasonableness of the time fixed by the notice must be judged as at the date when it is given. If it is reasonable, and the contractor does not fulfil his obligations within the new time stipulated, then the employer will have the right to terminate. However, where the employer leads the contractor to believe that he will not insist on time being of the essence, he cannot afterwards set up the original condition as to time.

Peak v McKinney (1970)

The facts of this case are set out above. The contract in question contained extension of time and liquidated damages provisions, as well as a clause stating that 'time shall be considered as of the essence of the contract on the part of the contractor'.

Salmon LJ was highly critical of the drafting of the contract, describing the same as being worthy of a prize for 'the most one-sided, obscurely and ineptly drafted clauses in the United Kingdom'. However, the Court of Appeal did not object to the principle of upholding an employer's right to terminate pursuant to a time of the essence clause even where the contract contained extension of time and liquidated damages provisions, with Salmon LJ expressing 'no doubt' that the employer would be entitled to terminate if the contract period (as extended) had expired.

J M Hill & Sons v London Borough of Camden (1980)

The claimant contractors were engaged by the defendant for the construction of housing in Camden. The contract was bespoke but largely took the form of the *JCT Standard Form of*

Building Contract (1963 edition). The contractor pulled the majority of its labour from site, but left supervisory staff and nominated subcontractors, when the employer failed to pay promptly against three interim certificates. Notices subsequently crossed each other in the post: the first from the contractor (following a warning letter one week previously) determining its employment for non-payment, and the second from the employer threatening to determine the contractor's employment as a result of the contractor's failure to proceed regularly and diligently with the works. The Court held that the contractor's notices were lawful, and that even though it had reduced its labour so as not to be proceeding 'regularly and diligently' with the works (as required by the contract (and clause 25 of the *JCT* form), its conduct was not repudiatory, as the contractor's conduct suggested that it was treating the contract as still subsisting.

Lombard South Central Plc v Butterworth (1987)

The defendant was the lessee of a computer under a contract of hire made with the claimant in 1981. The contract contained a term requiring punctual payment of each quarterly rental payment was 'to the essence' of the contract. The first two instalments under the contract were made promptly, but the next three were late. The claimant terminated the contract and retook possession of the computer. The Court of Appeal held that where a contract contains a condition making time is of the essence, a party will have the right of determination if that condition is breached, irrespective of the magnitude of the other party's breach. Thus, it would appear that an employer under a construction contract containing such a term would be empowered to eject the contractor from site even if the delays are minor.

Balfour Beatty Building Ltd v Chestermount Properties Ltd (1993)

In this case, Colman J provided a valuable interpretation of clause 25 of the *JCT Standard Form of Building Contract*, stating that the purpose of the power to grant an extension of time under clause 25.3 was to fix the period of time by which the period of time available for completion ought to be extended having regard to the incidence of the relevant events, measured by the standard of what is fair and reasonable.

Bedfordshire County Council v Fitzpatrick (1998)

The defendant contractors were engaged by the claimant council to carry out a rolling programme of maintenance works to highways in Bedfordshire. The date for commencement was 1 June 1996. the defendant sought to defer the start date after becoming worried about the true amount of work under the contract. No agreement was reached and 1 June passed without any works taking place. Accordingly, the claimant provided a notice to the defendant stating that unless works commenced by 15 June 1996, the defendant's employment would be terminated. On 15 June 1995, the council terminated the defendant's employment. On the facts, the Court held that it was unreasonable to require the contractors to commence work on 15 June: in the circumstances, the contractors harboured genuine concerns about the level of work, the amount of work to be carried out prior to 15 June was minimal, and the council was aware that the contractors were willing to fulfil its contractual obligations, subject to a delayed start.

Shawton Engineering Ltd v DGP International Ltd (2006)

The facts of this case are set out above. The Court of Appeal confirmed that an employer could legitimately terminate a contractor's employment on the grounds of delay on two bases:

(i) if a completion date fixed in a reasonable notice making time of the essence was not complied with; and/or

(ii) if the failure to complete works within a reasonable time was so flagrant that It effectively deprived the innocent party substantially of the whole benefit of the contract.

In respect of (i) above, the Court of Appeal further ruled that a party seeking to make time of the essence is required to demonstrate that the other party was in breach of its time obligations under the contract at the time of the notice purporting to make time of the essence.

Summary

- In building contracts, time will not be of the essence unless the contract so provides. Thus, an employer will not be permitted to determine a dilatory contractor's employment under the contract unless the delay is manifest and amounts to a repudiation.
- The existence of contractual provisions to extend time and require the payment of liquidated damages militates against time being of the essence in that contract. However, even where such clauses are present, there appears to be nothing wrong in principle with the insertion of an additional provision making time of the essence.
- Absent a contractual term, an employer may, when the contractor is already in breach of his time obligations, make time of the essence going forward by the serving of an appropriate notice on the contractor. Essentially, by the service of such a notice, the employer informs the contractor that he will treat further delay as repudiatory.
- Whether or not such a notice will be effective will depend on whether on the facts it was reasonable to make time of the essence *per se*, and whether the period allowed for completion in the time of the essence notice was reasonable.

4.6 CONCURRENT DELAY

Although there are no special principles in respect of the question of causation in construction contracts, the general rule is that a claimant must attribute his losses to a an event or events which is/are the legal responsibility of the defendant ('a defendant event') (see *McAlpine Humberoak v McDermott International* (1992) 58 BLR 1, CA).

In analysing a contractor's entitlement to an extension of time, difficulties will arise where causes of delay to a building project are said to be 'concurrent': i.e. where there are two or more competing causes of delay.

It goes without saying that each claim or group of claims in respect of delay must be examined on its own facts. It is frequently the case that the causative potency of genuinely concurrent events will often be different and, as a matter of fact, one particular cause will emerge as being critical. In practice, true concurrency is relatively rare.

The law surrounding concurrent delay is complicated and has been the subject of considerable academic scrutiny (see, for example, *Keating on Construction Contracts* (8th edition) at 8-015-8-022, and John Marrin QC, 'Concurrent Delay' (2002) 18 Const L.J., 436). In this section, two of the key authorities are summarised insofar as they deal with contracts containing express provisions for extensions of time and 'relevant events', and which are generally regarded as stating the current position.

Henry Boot Construction (UK) Ltd v Malmaison Hotel (Manchester) Ltd (1999)

Pursuant to a *JCT Standard Form of Building Contract (1980 edition)*, the claimant contractor was engaged by the defendant to construct the Malmaison hotel in Manchester. Extensions of time were granted by the architect taking the date for completion from 21 November 1997 to 6 January 1998. Practical completion was not achieved until 13 March 1998. A dispute arose over the cause of the delay, the contractor claiming that it was impeded by nominated subcontractors, and the employer retorting that this was not causative of delay, or if it was, such delay was caused by the claimant's failure to provide proper access to the subcontractor. The contractor further claimed that he had a valid extension of time claim resulting from late or inadequate instructions from the architect. The dispute was referred to arbitration. It came before the Court on jurisdictional grounds.

The Court held that any one delay or period of delay may, as a matter of causation, be attributed to more than one delaying event. Thus, an architect might legitimately grant a contractor an extension of time in the event of inclement weather, despite the fact that during that same period, the contractor could not mobilise sufficient labour to properly effect works on site; the operative cause is determined by the allocation of risk between the parties according to the provisions of the contract:

> '... it is agreed that if there are two concurrent causes of delay, one of which is a relevant event, and the other is not, then the Contractor is entitled to an extension of time for the period of delay caused by the relevant event notwithstanding the concurrent effect of the other event. Thus, to take a simple example, if no work is possible on our site for a week not only because of exceptionally inclement weather (a relevant event), but also because the Contractor has a shortage of labour (not a relevant event), and if the failure to work during that week is likely to delay the works beyond the Completion Date by one week, then if he considers it fair and reasonable to do so, the Architect is required to grant an extension of time of one week ...'

Royal Brompton Hospital NHS Trust v Hammond and Others (No. 7) (2001)

This case was one of many disputes arising out of the refurbishment of the Royal Brompton Hospital in Chelsea, London. *No. 7* was a professional negligence action brought against the defendant architects on the grounds that they had been too generous in awarding extensions of time under the contract. The Court was thus not directly concerned with the issue of whether extensions of time should or should not be granted in cases of true concurrency. However, in delivering his judgment (and approving the approach of Dyson J in *Malmaison*) HHJ Seymour QC made it clear that true concurrency was certainly not a frequent occurrence:

> '... it is, I think, necessary to be clear what one means by events operating concurrently. It does not mean, in my judgment, a situation in which, work already being delayed, let it be supposed, because the Contractor has had difficulty in obtaining sufficient labour, an event occurs which is a relevant event and which, had the Contractor not been delayed, would have caused him to be delayed, but which in fact by reason of the existing delay, made no difference. In such a situation although there is a relevant event, "the completion of the works is [not] likely to be delayed thereby beyond the Completion Date".'

Time for completion and extensions of time

It is also useful to consider cases dealt with under Global Claims, below, which explore a number of related concepts.

4.7 OWNERSHIP OF THE 'FLOAT'

'Float' is essentially extra time built into the contractor's programme over and above that which is required to complete any particular activity. The issue of 'ownership' of the float will arise where delay to a construction project causes a knock-on effect resulting in a delay to the completion date through no fault of the contractor.

Where there is a delay in the completion date by reason of the employer's tardiness, contractors argue that they have a right to an extension of time to make up for the delay. In response, employers argue that the float is a matter for the contractor alone and that in any event the project should be completed by the completion date.

The relevant question is therefore: who has ownership of the float? If it is the contractor, he may (in principle) be entitled to claim an extension of time and/or loss and expense. If it is the employer, the existence of the float will be irrelevant: the contractor simply has to complete to time and no allowance will be made for the pre-existence of breathing space in the construction programme. If this is the case, then a contractor will be deprived of the benefit of its contingency plan (i.e. the float) through no fault of its own.

4.7.1 Position under JCT

The mechanics of *JCT* have curious consequences in respect of 'float', which stem from the fact that the *JCT* forms do not recognise the concept. Thus, where initial delays are caused to a project on account of variations or 'employer events' such as problems with accessing the site, or late supply of design information, such matters will not be causative of delay to the completion date as they are absorbed by the 'float'. Obviously, the order in which 'contractor' and 'employer' delaying events occur is impossible to predict and is outwith the control of the contractor.

The Royal Brompton Hospital NHS Trust v Frederick Alexander Hammond and others (2002)

Per HHJ Havery QC:

> 'Under the JCT conditions, as used here, there can be no doubt that if an architect is required to form an opinion then, if there is then unused float for the benefit of the contractor (and not for another reason such as to deal with p.c. or provisional sums or items), then the architect is bound to take it into account since an extension is only to be granted if completion would otherwise be delayed beyond the then current completion date. This may seem hard to a contractor but the objects of an extension of time clause are to avoid the contractor being liable for liquidated damages where there has been delay for which it is not responsible, and still to establish a new completion date to which the contractor should work so that both the employer and the contractor know where they stand. The architect should in such circumstances inform the contractor that, if thereafter events occur for which an extension of time cannot be granted, and if, as a result, the contractor would be liable for liquidated damages then an appropriate extension, not exceeding the float, would be given. In that way the purposes of the clause can be met: the date for completion is always known; the position on liquidated damages is clear; yet the contractor is not deprived permanently of "its" float. Under these JCT Conditions the Architect cannot revise an extension once given so as to fix an earlier date (except in the limited circumstances set out in clauses 25.3.2 and 25.3.3). Thus to grant an extension which preserved the contractor's float would not be "fair and reasonable". Under clause 23.1 the employer is entitled to completion on or before the Completion Date so the employer is ultimately entitled to the benefit of any unused float that the contractor does not need. Few contractors wish to remain on a site any longer than is needed and employers are usually happy to take possession earlier, rather than later, and, if they are not, they have to accept the risk of early completion. In practice however architects are not normally concerned about these points and may reasonably take the view that, unless the float is obvious, its existence need not be discovered.'

4.7.2 Position under NEC3

In an *NEC3* contract, the programme is revised periodically (generally monthly) with the consequence that projected completion dates for each stage are continually being assessed and reassessed. The hope is that, as a result, float is much less likely to be a point of contention due to the fact that it will be continually revised and float (providing of course that it is properly disclosed) will be protected when changes are made to the completion date.

Summary

- Whilst the position is not clear under the *JCT* form, the decision in *Brompton v Hammond* suggests that the float is owned by the project whilst possibly also building in a level of protection for the forward-thinking contractor.
- It may be possible to prevent any potential 'injustice' over ownership of float by inserting an express condition into the contract which stipulated that the contractor's float must be taken into consideration and preserved when considering any award for extension of time.

5
Liquidated damages

5.1 INTRODUCTION

As has been seen, proving the causes of delay to a building project may be a complicated exercise. Proving the consequences of such delay in financial terms may be equally fraught with difficulty. If a contractor suffers loss as a result of delay, it will be incumbent on him to prove such losses in the normal manner (as to which, see Chapter 6). The position vis-à-vis an employer, however, is often different, courtesy of particular provisions frequently incorporated into building contracts providing that the employer's damages occasioned by delay are 'liquidated'. Such clauses are often referred to in shorthand as 'LDs' (liquidated damages) clauses or 'LADs' (liquidated and ascertained damages) clauses, and such liquidated damages may either be set off against or deducted from sums owing to the contractor if the contract allows.

One important purpose of liquidated damages clauses is that they allow the parties, from the outset, to know where they stand if works run into delay. In other words, by including such a provision, the contractor knows the extent of his delay liability and agrees to it.

Further, providing that the figure inserted in the LAD provision is indeed a genuine pre-estimation of the employer's loss occasioned by delay (as to which, see below) it will save valuable time and expense in having to prove such matters before a tribunal.

Clydebank Engineering and Shipbuilding Company Ltd v Don Jose Ramos Yzquierdo y Castenada (1905)

This case concerned the construction of four torpedo vessels for the Spanish Government. Late delivery was to be penalised under the contract at a rate of £500 per week. Lord

Halsbury held that it was 'obvious on the face of the contract that the very thing intended to be provided against by this pactional amount of damages is to avoid kind of minute and somewhat difficult and complex system of examination that would be necessary if you were to attempt to prove the damage'.

However, as is explored below, circumstances will arise in which an LAD clause fetters the extent of the employer's recovery or may even be deemed unenforceable. In such circumstances, an employer may be forced to prove his actual (i.e. unliquidated) losses, sometimes referred to as 'delay damages', at common law. Conversely, depending on the wording of the contract, in certain circumstances, an employer may lose his right to claim LADs, or delay damages, or both.

5.2 THE *CONTRA PROFERENTEM* RULE

Peak Construction (Liverpool) Ltd v McKinney (1970)

The facts of this case are set out in Chapter 4 above. In that case, Salmon LJ held that where a form of contract had been devised by an employer, an LAD provision should be construed 'strictly *contra proferentem*'.

Tersons Ltd v Stevenage Development Corporation (1977)

The claimant contractors entered into a contract to furnish and lay certain pipe sewers pursuant to the *General Conditions of Contract and Forms of Tender, Agreement and Bond for use in connection with Works of Civil Engineering Construction (2nd edition, January, 1950)*. The claimant contended that clause 52 of that contract, which dealt with payment in the event of the ordering of additional work, should be construed against the corporation. Pearson LJ confirmed that the *contra preferentem* maxim did not automatically apply to industry-wide standard form contracts:

> 'Mr Kerr has contended that the maxim *verba accipiuntur fortius contra proferentem* should be applied in this case in favour of the contractor against the Corporation on the ground that the General Conditions were included in the invitation to tender sent by the Corporation to the

contractor. In my view, the maxim has little, if any, application in this case. The General Conditions are not a partisan document or an "imposed standard contract" as that phrase is sometimes used. It was not drawn up by one party in its own interests and imposed on the other party. It is a general form, evidently in common use, and prepared and revised jointly by several representative bodies including the Federation of Civil Engineering Contractors. It would naturally be incorporated in a contract of this kind, and should have the same meaning whether the one party or the other happens to have made the first mention of it in the negotiations.'

R W Green Ltd v Cade Bros Farms (1978)

A similar view was taken of an industry standard form terms, which are not readily susceptible to a *contra proferentem* construction. The Court held that the contract, like any commercial contract, must be considered and construed against the background of the trade in which it operates. The conditions were based upon a standard form of conditions produced by the National Association of Seed Potato Merchants, and used by a large majority of seed potato merchants for over 20 years. They had evolved over a much longer period as the result both of trade practice and discussions between the Association and the National Farmers' Union. They were therefore not conditions imposed by the strong upon the weak; but were rather a set of trading terms upon which both sides were apparently content to do business.

McAlpine v Tilebox (2005)

In this recent decision of the TCC, which is discussed in more detail below, Jackson J stated that the courts are generally predisposed to uphold a contractual term which sets the level of damages for breach especially where the contact is between parties of comparable bargaining power. See Chapter 4 above.

Murray v Leisureplay (2005)

Following a thorough review of the authorities, the Court of Appeal emphasised the need for legal certainty and stated

Liquidated damages

that the Court should give weight to the fact that the parties have agreed the particular clause. Clarke LJ affirmed that the courts should be cautious before holding that a clause in a contract of this kind is a penalty.

Summary

- The 'traditional' approach of the courts is to construe LAD clauses *contra proferentem*.
- Such an interpretation does not appear to be favoured by the Courts when industry standard form contracts are used.
- More recent jurisprudence seems to indicate a movement away from a strict application of the 'traditional' approach, especially where the contract is between two commercial parties.

5.3 THE OPERABLE EXTENT OF AN LAD CLAUSE

Cellulose Acetate v Widnes Foundry (1933)

The contractors were engaged by the defendants to deliver and install an acetone recovery plant. The contract contained a liquidated damages clause of £20 per week for every week that the construction was delayed beyond the completion date. Completion was finally achieved 30 weeks late. The contractors claimed for the contract price; the defendants claimed for the actual loss that they had suffered as a result of the late completion, namely £5,850. The House of Lords held that the contractors were liable for the sum of £600 and no more.

Surrey Heath Borough Council v Lovell Construction Ltd (1988)

The claimant council engaged the defendant contractor to design and build new offices at Camberley, Surrey, pursuant to a *JCT Standard Form of Building Contract (1981 edition)*, with contractor's design. During the carrying out of the project, an extensive fire occurred following the carrying out of welding operations. The fire was negligently caused, and severely damaged the works, delaying the project by some 18 months. The Court held that whether the failure to meet the contractual completion date was caused by a breach of contract (such as causing a fire) or simply from failing to proceed regularly and diligently with the works, the employer's remedy for any losses caused by the delay would be the same, i.e. the payment of liquidated damages.

M J Gleeson plc v Taylor Woodrow Construction Ltd (1989)

The defendant management contractor entered into a subcontract with the claimant in respect of works to be carried out to the Imperial War Museum, London. Delays occurred to the works. The contract contained an LAD clause at a rate of £400/week. The subcontract further provided (at clause 11) that if the claimant failed to complete the subcontract works on time, it would pay the defendant 'a sum equivalent to any direct loss damage or expense suffered or incurred by' [the defendant], including such loss or damage 'suffered or incurred by any other sub-contractor for which [the defendant] is or may be liable under the relevant subcontract.' The defendant sought to set off two sums against sums owing to the claimant, the first being liquidated damages (pursuant to the liquidated damages clause) and the second for 'set-off claims' of ten other subcontractors (pursuant to clause 11).

HHJ Davies QC held that the 'set-off claims' were attributable to the claimant's failure to complete the works on time, and thus fell to be included in the liquidated damages set-off. Claiming both amounted to a 'double deduction'.

Pigott Foundations v Shepherd Construction (1993)

The claimant was a specialist piling contractor who was engaged by the defendant main contractor in respect of the construction of an office block in Coventry. The piles proved to be unsatisfactory and additional piles had to be installed. Instead of completing works by August 1989, Pigott did not leave site until October 1989. A particular clause incorporated into the contract between the parties provided that 'damages would only apply in the event of Pigott's not completing within 10 weeks and any sum would be limited to £40,000 (max) at the rate of £10,000 per week.' The Court held that this liquidated damages provision was an exhaustive agreement in respect of damages for non-completion or delay.

The maximum limit set by such a provision could not be sidestepped by claiming general damages for delay resulting from a breach of any other provision of the contract.

Summary

Although it will be a matter of construction in each case, the court will readily construe an LAD clause so that it covers all of the employer's losses occasioned by the contractor's delay.

5.4 THE OPERATION OF THE 'PREVENTION PRINCIPLE'

The 'prevention principle' has already been discussed in Chapter 4 above. Its application in relation to LAD provisions is as important as it is to extension of time clauses (and often the two will be inextricably interlinked).

Peak v McKinney (1970)

This case has been considered above in Chapter 4. The Court further held that where any part of the delay to the works had been caused by the employer in circumstances where no extension of time was due there could be no liability for liquidated damages.

The editors of *Keating on JCT Contracts* (at 1.1-113) suggest that a contract administrator may be under a duty to advise the employer of this principle of law if it becomes apparent that it might apply during the course of construction works. Should the employer withhold payment on erroneous grounds that liquidated damages are payable, then the contractor has an express right to terminate the contract.

SMK Cabinets v Hili Modern Electrics (1984)

The defendant was an electrical contracting company which entered into a contract with the claimant to carry out the installation of cabinets to a property. Completion was required by 15 July 1980, but no extension of time clause was incorporated into the contract. The contract contained a liquidated damages provision of $35/day for every day that the works remained incomplete, which would begin to bite seven days after the completion date (i.e. after 22 July 1980). By December 1980, the works were still not complete, and the defendant sought to determine the contract. The claimant resisted the payment of liquidated damages on the grounds that the defendant company had prevented completion by 22 July 1980 as a result of variations and interference with the smooth progress of the works. On the facts, an arbitrator had found that the contractor would, in any event, have been unable to complete by the due date. The Supreme Court of Victoria held that this was irrelevant. Accordingly, the contractor was not liable to pay liquidated damages on account of the prevention, even though he would not have achieved timely completion even if the prevention had not taken place. (It is submitted that this authority is consistent with the approach of the courts in allowing an extension of time to a contractor where concurrent delay is caused by a relevant event and the contractor's own default. See Chapter 4.)

McAlpine Humberoak v McDermott International (1992)

The claimant was a contractor engaged by the defendant to supply and install steel parts for an oil platform off the Shetland Islands. From the outset, the works fell into delay, with both parties blaming each other for the same. Extra work was ordered by the defendant towards the end of the construction process, on 11 June 1982.

The Court of Appeal held the claimant responsible for the majority of the delay and, notwithstanding the late instruction of additional work, the claimant was only entitled to an extension of time until 30 April 1982 (i.e. prior to the instruction of that additional work). Lloyd LJ put the point succinctly as follows:

> 'If a contractor is already a year late through his culpable fault, it would be absurd that the employer should lose his claim for unliquidated damages just because, at the last moment, he orders an extra coat of paint.'

If prevention occurs after completion date and contractor is already in delay, can recover liquidated damages up to date of prevention and possibly beyond.

Jones v St John's College Oxford (1870)

The claimant was a building contractor who agreed to complete certain works by a certain date, subject to alterations or additions which might be made. Liquidated damages were set at £3/day. The Court held that the contract was an 'absolute' contract, namely that, upon a proper interpretation of its terms, the contractor had undertaken to carry out all of the works, including any extra works ordered by the employer, within the time originally limited. The Court held that, in the circumstances, liquidated damages were recoverable. In other words, the employer may, by his actions, have prevented the completion of the contract works by the contract date, but provided that the contract provides for and exonerates such an eventuality, liquidated damages will nonetheless be payable.

Rapid Building v Ealing Family Housing (1984)

The claimants were building contractors who were responsible for the construction of a housing estate in West London. Possession of the site was delayed past the contractual date for the same as a result of squatters. Works commenced late and were not completed until 26 July 1983, after the contractual date for completion. The architect issued a certificate stating that the works should reasonably have been completed by 22 September 1982.

The Court ruled that the defendants' failure to give possession of the site was a breach of contract, and applied *Peak v McKinney*, holding that the defendants' counterclaim for liquidated damages could not succeed as the contract did not provide a mechanism for extending time for that particular breach of contract. In such circumstances, time is at large, and the employer is permitted to recover unliquidated damages if the contractor does not complete the works within a reasonable time.

Summary

- In general terms, if the employer is responsible for delay, he cannot claim liquidated damages for failure to complete the works by the date specified in the contract,

Case in Point – Construction Claims

and time will be at large, apparently even if the contractor would not have completed to time in any event.

- The position will be different if the employer causes delay that prevents timely completion, but the employer validly extends time in respect of delay for which he is responsible. Liquidated damages will then be recoverable from the revised completion date.

- The contractor fails to apply for an appropriate extension of time in accordance with the relevant contractual preconditions. In such circumstances, the contractor may still be liable for liquidated damages even though he has not caused delay (see Chapter 4).

- The employer's act of prevention occurs after the completion date. Liquidated damages will then be recoverable up to the date of prevention.

- The contract is 'absolute'. Liquidated damages will then be recoverable even if the employer orders variations so as to delay the completion of the works. It is suggested that this is an unlikely scenario in modern construction projects.

5.5 PENALTY CLAUSES

As illustrated by the cases selected below, in the construction context, an LAD provision will be enforced so long as it constitutes a genuine pre-estimate of the employer's loss occasioned by the contractor's delay. If the amount claimed in the LAD clause is excessive, the court may refuse to enforce it on the grounds that it is penal. There is much case law on the topic: useful summaries can be found in the speech of Mance LJ in *Cine Bes Filmcilik Ve Yapim Click v UIP* [2003] EWCA Civ 1699 and in *McAlpine v Tilebox* (see below).

Dunlop Pneumatic Tyre Company v New Garage and Motor Company Ltd (1915)

In this leading case, Lord Dunedin reviewed the authorities on the 'penalty clause' doctrine and distilled the same into a set of four principles, which are still commonly relied upon today. The contract in question was between a manufacturer and dealer of Dunlop tyres, which contained a clause

Liquidated damages

requiring the payment of £5 for every tyre sold in breach of contract, below list price, or to persons blacklisted by Dunlop.

1. Though the parties to a contract who use the word 'penalty' or 'liquidated damages' may prima facie be supposed to mean what they say, yet the expression used is not conclusive. The Court must find out whether the payment stipulated is in truth penalty or liquidated damages. This doctrine may be said to be found passim in nearly every case.

2. The essence of a penalty is a payment of money stipulated as in terrorem of the offending party; the essence of liquidated damages is a genuine covenanted pre-estimate of damage.

3. The question whether a sum stipulated is penalty or liquidated damages is a question of construction to be decided upon the terms and inherent circumstances of each particular contract, judged as at the time of making the contract, not as at the time of the breach.

4. To assist this task of construction various tests have been suggested, which if applicable to the case under consideration, may prove helpful, or even inclusive. Such are:

    (a) It will be held to be a penalty if the sum stipulated for is extravagant and unconscionable in amount in comparison with the greatest loss that could conceivably be proved to have followed from the breach.

    (b) It will be held to be a penalty if the breach consists only in not paying a sum of money, and the sum stipulated is a sum greater than the sum which ought to have been paid. This, though one of the most ancient instances, is truly a corollary to the last test.

    (c) There is a presumption (but no more) that it is a penalty when 'A single lump sum is made payable by way of compensation, on the occurrence of one or more or all of several events, some of which may occasion serious and others but trifling damage'.

    On the other hand:

(d) It is no obstacle to the sum stipulated being a genuine pre-estimate of damage, that the consequences of the breach are such as to make precise pre-estimation almost an impossibility on. On the contrary, that is just the situation when it is probable that pre-estimate damage was the true bargain between the parties.

Clydebank Engineering Co v Yzquierdo y Castaneda (1905)

In this case, which concerned the construction of torpedo vessels for the Spanish government, the underlying contract contained a provision which was described as a 'penalty' clause for non-completion to time. The House of Lords upheld the provision on the basis that is was a genuine LAD clause. Though the parties to a contract who use the word 'penalty' or 'liquidated damages' may prima facie be supposed to mean what they say, the expression used is not conclusive.

Philips Hong Kong Ltd v AG of Hong Kong (1993)

The claimant was one of seven contractors with the Government of Hong Kong for the design, supply , installation and supervision of a processor-based supervisory system for the approach roads and twin tube tunnels of a major highway. The appendix to the contract provided for liquidated damages to be payable in the event that certain key dates were missed, and for failing to complete the whole of the works within the time specified. The amount of liquidated damages payable for failure to meet a key date varied according to which key date was missed. The claimant sought a declaration that the relevant clause was unenforceable, succeeding at first instance. Eventually the Privy Council dismissed the claimant's case, stating that:

1   The test for deciding whether a liquidated damages clause is penal is to consider whether or not it is a genuine pre-estimate of what the loss is likely to be.
2   A liquidated damages clause will not be penal simply because there may be situations in which the clause's application might result in recovery over and above actual loss suffered:

Liquidated damages

'...it will normally be insufficient to establish that a provision is objectionably penal to identify situations where the application of the provision could result in a larger sum being recovered by the injured party than his actual loss. Even in such situations so long as the sum payable in the event of non-compliance with the contract is not extravagant, having regard to the range of losses that it could reasonable by anticipated it would have to cover at the time the contract was made, it can still be a genuine pre-estimate of the loss that would be suffered and so a perfectly valid liquidated damages provision.' Per Lord Woolf at 58-59.

3   An employer, in pre-estimating liquidated damages, should carefully consider the types of losses which might arise and factor these into any formula it uses.

4   A minimum payment provision is not penal if it can be reasonably assumed that a delay in completion will inevitably continue to incur expenses irrespective of the scale of work.

Jeancharm Ltd (t/a Beaver International) v Barnet Football Club Ltd (2003)

The claimant had contracted to supply the defendant's football kit for two seasons. Under the agreement, if the claimant was late in delivering the kit, it was obliged to pay over 20 pence per garment per day. If the defendant was late in paying, it was obliged to pay interest at the rate of 5per cent per week. In performing the contract, disputes arose in relation to late delivery and late payment.

On appeal, the Court of Appeal considered whether the interest clause (which amounted to an annual rate of 260 per cent) constituted a penalty clause. The Court rejected the claimant's submission that the Privy Council's decision in *Phillips Hong Kong Ltd v The Attorney General of Hong Kong* heralded an abandonment of Lord Dunedin's statement of the law in *Dunlop v New Garage*, finding instead that (after *Phillips*) the courts must take care in assessing whether a clause is a genuine pre-estimate of damage when the parties are of equal bargaining power. Accordingly, the interest clause was a penalty clause, and thus unenforceable.

Murray v Leisureplay (2005)

Mr Murray was an employee of the defendant company pursuant to a retainer which was determined by the defendant in disputed circumstances. Mr Murray contended that he had been wrongfully dismissed, thus entitling him to the payment of one year's salary pursuant to a 'liquidated damages' clause in the retainer (clause 17) The defendant alleged that clause 17 was penal and unenforceable. Having reviewed the authorities, Arden LJ suggested that a five-fold test was appropriate when approaching the question of whether or not an LAD clause will amount to a penalty:

1   To what breaches of contract does the contractual damages provision apply?
2   What amount is payable on breach under that clause in the parties' agreement?
3   What amount would be payable if a claim for damages for breach of contract was brought under common law?
4   What were the parties' reasons for agreeing for the relevant clause?
5   Has the party who seeks to establish that the clause is a penalty shown that the amount payable under the clause was imposed in terrorem, or that it does not constitute a genuine pre-estimate of loss...and, if he has shown the latter, is there some other reason which justifies the discrepancy between 2 and 3 above?

The Court of Appeal concluded that if an employer can recover more pursuant to an LAD clause than his actual proven loss, it may lead to conclusion that the clause is penal; equally it may not. Greater recovery may be justifiable on commercial grounds, i.e. to discourage the other party from breaching its contractual obligations. In the circumstances, the Court of Appeal ruled that clause 17 was not penal, drawing on (for example) the 'fierce restrictions on competition' imposed on Mr Murray by the contract, and the advantage to the defendant of avoiding wasting money on management time or lawyers' fees in working out the damages to be paid at common law in the event of a breach of the contract of employment.

Buxton LJ considered that the underlying principle of *Dunlop* could be recast in modern terms as a requirement that the LAD clause should be compensatory rather than deterrent. He went on to say (at 116):

> 'It is therefore necessary to stand back and look at the reality of this agreement. Although I agree that evidence about it is sparse, I am prepared to take judicial notice of the fact that an entrepreneurial company such as MFC...will often place a high value upon retaining the services, and the loyalty and attention, of that one man as its chief executive: to the extent of including in his "package" generous reassurance against the eventuality of dismissal. That such reassurance exceeds the likely amount of contractual damages on dismissal does not render the terms penal unless the party seeking to avoid the terms can demonstrate that they meet the test of extravagance posited by Lord Dunedin and by Lord Woolf.'

McAlpine v Tilebox (2005)

The defendant was a development company that engaged the claimant contractor to develop a property in Guildford into a 90,000 sq ft commercial premises suitable for a corporate headquarters. The contract, which took the form of the *JCT Standard Form of Building Contract with Contractor's Design (1998 edition)*, provided for liquidated damages to be payable at a rate of £45,000 per week. McAlpine claimed that this sum was penal; Tilebox retorted that its potential liability to the ultimate employer, Standard Life (including lost rental income and the erosion of Tilebox's completion payment under a pain/gain share mechanism) was included within the LAD clause and the provision was thus enforceable.

Jackson J, following a comprehensive analysis of the authorities, found that the LAD clause was a reasonable pre-estimate of losses and was actually lower than the actual losses suffered by Tilebox. On the facts, it was foreseeable that Tilebox's potential losses arising out of delay could include its liability to Standard Life in terms of lost rental income and its inability to recover all or part of its completion bonus.

In order to avoid an LAD provision, it was insufficient to show that payments recoverable under that provision are disproportionate to those allowable at common law: a substantial discrepancy is required between estimated loss and the LAD sum. Although the pre-estimate has to be genuine, the test to be applied is an objective test, and does not turn on the honesty or 'genuineness' of the employer who makes such a pre-estimate.

CFW Architects (a firm) v Cowlin Construction Ltd (2006)

This dispute concerned the construction of houses for military personnel in Tidworth, Wiltshire. The claimant architect was retained by the defendant contractor to carry out and coordinate the defendant's design package for the works. HHJ Thornton QC held that the claimant architects repudiated the contract, such repudiation being accepted by the defendant. The contractor sought to recover (amongst other things) a sum of over £400,000 representing liquidated damages which had been levied upon it by the employer pursuant to the *GC/Works/1 (edition 3) 1998 revision* standard form design and build contract between the employer and the contractor. The actual figure claimed by the contractor against the architect for liquidated damages was paid to the employer following a settlement between the employer and the contractor.

The design and build contract provided for liquidated damages calculated on a house-by-house basis. The houses were to be used for relocating military personnel and, as a result, the LAD provision expressly comprised (amongst other things) the cost of alternative accommodation for a six-month period (this being the minimum period in respect of which alternative accommodation could be organised).

The architect sought to avoid this head of loss on the grounds that the liquidated damages provision in that contract was penal, arguing that if (as was the case) an extension of time had been granted, then the employer would have had to enter into alternative rental arrangements in any event, and thus should not have passed on such costs to the contractor.

The Court held that whilst the liquidated damages provision was 'potentially harsh', it was nonetheless enforceable;

Liquidated damages

although it was not a certainty, it was possible that the alternative accommodation charges could arise at the point when liquidated damages first became payable (as opposed to arising in any event as a result of a delay for which the contractor was not responsible).

This appears to be a reformulation of the 'greatest loss that could conceivably be proved to have followed from the breach' principle as articulated by Lord Dunedin.

Watts v Mitsui (1917)

This case concerned a charterparty agreement for the provision of a steamer to load a cargo of sulphate of ammonia at Marioupol. The House of Lords held that the liquidated damages provision amounted to a penalty. In the circumstances, the employer has a choice of either claiming unliquidated damages or the actual loss which he proves up to the amount of the penalty.

Rapid Building v Ealing (1984)

The facts of this case are set out above. The claimants argued that the defendants could not recover more in unliquidated damages than the sum set out in the liquidated damages provision (which was ineffective). The Court did not decide this point: at the time of printing, in the construction context, at least, the issue is still unresolved.

The editors of *Keating on Construction Contracts* (8th edition, 2006) suggest (at 9-014) that the liquidated damages provision should operate as a 'limit' to the contractor's liability. However, *MacGregor on Damages* (17th edition) reaches the opposite conclusion at 13-020.

Summary

- In the construction context, when deciding whether an LAD clause is unenforceable as a penalty, the court must be satisfied that the clause in question is not a genuine pre-estimate of the employer's loss, to be judged at the time of contracting.
- It seems that only if the sum stipulated for is 'extravagant' compared to the greatest extent of the employer's potential

loss at common law at the time of contracting that an LAD clause will be held to be penal.
- The onus in proving that an LAD clause is penal will be on the party who contends that it is (usually the contractor).
- Whilst the parties' own terminology may be of some assistance, it is for the tribunal to establish whether the payment stipulated is in truth penalty or liquidated damages.
- Recent jurisprudence suggests that the courts will be slow to strike down an LAD clause as penal in circumstances where it has been agreed by two commercial parties, even if it seems unlikely that an employer could prove that his actual loss is as great as the amount stipulated in the LAD provision.
- Simply because an employer may recover more pursuant to an LAD provision than would be the case at common law, does not automatically lead to the conclusion that the provision is penal. The tribunal must look to the reasons why the clause was inserted and recognise the importance of commercial negotiations. The tribunal may also take into account the practical consequences of a wrongful termination if the LAD clause was *not* in the contract when arriving at its conclusions.

In the construction context, it is, as yet, undecided whether an employer can recover a greater sum at common law than the LAD provision would otherwise permit.

5.6 CONTRACTUAL PECULIARITIES

As is almost always the case in all building disputes, the terms of the underlying contract will provide the greatest assistance to the parties in terms of establishing the limits of the operation of the LAD provision. As with extension of time clauses (Chapter 4), the levying of LADs may be fettered or even prevented by the parties' failure to comply with formalities in the contract, or by the unsuitability of the contract to the case in point. Some of these scenarios are investigated in this section.

5.6.1 Entries against the appendix

Kemp v Rose (1858)

In this case, the date from which liquidated damages were to run was omitted from the contract documents. The oral evidence before the Court was contradictory as to the agreed completion date. In the circumstances, the Court refused to fix such a date, and held that liquidated damages were not payable. It is suggested that if oral evidence is clear (or agreed), and the omission was explained as an 'oversight', then the court may grant rectification in order to give effect to the parties' intentions and allow liquidated damages to be recoverable in principle.

Temloc Ltd v Errill Properties (1987)

In this case, which concerned the development of a shopping centre in Plymouth pursuant to the *JCT Standard Form of Building Contract (1980 edition)*, the parties had entered '£nil' in the liquidated damages section against clause 24.2 of the appendix of the JCT form. The Court of Appeal held that, on a proper construction of the contract, no damages would be recoverable for delayed completion (be they liquidated or unliquidated):

> 'I think it clear, both as a matter of construction and as onr of common sense, that if (1) clause 24 is incorporated in the contract and (2) the parties complete the relevant part of the appendix, either by stating a rate at which the sum is to be calculated or, as here, by stating that the sum is to be nil, then that constitutes an exhaustive agreement as to the damages which are, or are not, to be payable by the contractor in the event of his failure to complete the works on time.'

Whilst this decision is possibly surprising, it is possibly explicable on the evidence, during which the employer conceded that the sum '£nil' was entered as a 'bonus' in order to incentivise timely completion.

Baese Pty Ltd v R A Bracken (1989)

In this Australian case concerning the construction of a house on Australian JCC standard terms of contract, the liquidated damages for delay were stated as 'nil'. Practical completion was delayed by a month, and the claimant brought an action for interest charges levied against him during the extended period in which the works were incomplete. The defendant relied upon *Temloc v Errill* (see above). The Supreme Court of New South Wales refused to follow *Temloc v Errill*, stating that it was of no assistance as it was a contract on 'materially different terms', and allowed the recovery of unliquidated damages. The distinction can possibly be explained on the basis that it was more likely that no precise figure for LADs could be stated at the time of contracting, rather than evidencing the fact that the parties envisaged that no damages would be payable for delay.

5.6.2 The problem of sectional completion

Bramall & Ogden v Sheffield CC (1983) 1 Con LR 30

The dispute between the claimant contractor and the defendant concerned the defendant's right to deduct liquidated damages and the extensions of time granted pursuant to a *JCT Standard Form, 1963 edition* contract for the construction of 123 dwellings. Clause 16(e) provided for a reduced sum to be payable after taking partial possession while the appendix provided for the award of liquidated damages 'at the rate of £20 per week for each uncompleted dwelling.' The date for completion was stated as 6 December 1976 and the final practical completion certificate awarded for each section of buildings taken over was given on 20 September 1978. No formal sectional completion agreement was entered into. The defendant kept back £26,150 in liquidated damages.

The Court, on appeal from an arbitrator's decision, found that in the absence of any provision for sectional completion the defendant was not entitled to claim or deduct liquidated damages as provided in the appendix.

It was held that the contract did not provide for sectional completion, that the defendant had taken possession under clause 16(e), but that clause 16(e) was inconsistent with the liquidated damages appendix, so was unenforceable. (It is noteworthy that the Court relied on the *contra preferentem* principle in arriving at this conclusion. It may be that, in the light of modern jurisprudence, the case would be decided differently today.)

Bruno Zornow (Builders) v Beechcroft Developments (1989)

This dispute concerned preliminary works for a housing development carried out under the *JCT Standard Form of Building Contract, 1963 edition (1977 revision)*. The date for possession was set as 10 June 1985 with completion by 10 August 1985. The original works programme provided for payment of liquidated damages in the sum of £200/week for each block from the date when it ought to have been completed.

Following the commencement of works, a revised construction programme was sent which expanded the scope of works and provided that the same should be carried out in two phases, the first to complete in May 1986 and the second in November 1986. Completion occurred in December 1986, and extensions of time were granted to July 1986 and December 1986 for each phase respectively. The architect held back liquidated damages in the sum of £40,000, using the liquidated damages provision relating to the original (unphased) construction programme. The Court refused to imply a term for sectional completion dates, and no liquidated damages were payable.

Stanor Electric v R Mansell (1988)

The parties entered into a contract for the construction of two houses, which contained a provision for liquidated damages in respect of late completion of both properties. One of the houses was completed late, and the employer sought to deduct a part of the liquidated damages sum to reflect its late completion. The Court held that absent any contractual mechanisms entitling the employer to unilaterally reduce the amount of the LAD clause in this way, no liquidated damages could be claimed.

CFW Architects (a firm) v Cowlin Construction Ltd (2006)

The facts of this case are set out above.

After commencement of the works, the contractor introduced a further phasing arrangement for the houses, but this never became part of the contract. The employer refused to take over houses in accordance with the phasing arrangements, and instead insisted on taking possession only when the development was complete. In delivering his judgment, HHJ Thornton QC did not suggest that this would have precluded the recovery of liquidated damages. However, in line with the authorities above, it seems that if the employer had taken modified phased possession of the houses, it may have encountered difficulties in enforcing the LAD provision. (This is so even though the clause in question provided for completion on a house by house basis (as did the LAD clause in *Bruno Zornow*). However, given that the contract in *CFW v Cowlin* provided for phased completion in any event (as opposed to the contract in *Bruno Zornow* which did not), it is possible that a court could construe a 'modification' of that phasing as compatible with the underlying LAD provision. Caution should be exercised in circumstances where an employer may wish to either introduce or modify a sectional completion provision during a building project whilst also intending to preserve his right to claim liquidated damages.)

5.6.3 Contractual preconditions to recovery

Bell & Son (Paddington) Ltd v CBF Residential Care and Housing Association (1989)

The claimant contractor entered into a contract with the defendant for the construction of an extension to a building. The agreement was in the *JCT Standard Form of Building Contract, 1980 Private edition with Quantities* and liquidated damages for non-completion were stated to be at the rate of £700 per week. Under clause 24, the architect was required to issue a certificate if the contractor failed to complete the works by the completion date upon which the employer could inform the contractor in writing of its intention to subtract liquidated damages. A series of extensions of time were duly granted, for one of which a certificate and notice were issued, but after fixing a completion date of 20 May 1986, no further certificate was given until the final certificate on 25 April 1988. The defendant withheld £4,900 in liquidated damages, for which amount the claimant applied for summary judgment.

The Court, finding for the claimant, held that the correct construction of the contract required a certificate to be issued when a contractor failed to complete the works by the completion date and that a notice was superseded along with the certificate to which it applied. A certificate and notice were conditions precedent to the award of liquidated damages and in this instance neither had been given.

JF Finnegan Ltd v Community HA Ltd (1995)

The claimant was a contractor employed by the defendant to build 18 flats under a *JCT Standard Form of Building Contract 1980 Private edition with Quantities*. A dispute arose over the deduction of liquidated damages, which the Defendant did having issued a certificate and given written notice in a form which the Court at first instance found to be inadequate.

The Court of Appeal, finding for the defendant, held that:

1 Written notice by the employer is a condition precedent to the deduction of liquidated damages under the contract.
2 Written notice can be given at the same time as the deduction is made.
3 Written notice has to make clear that liquidated damages are being deducted and the extent of those liquidated damages. There is no need to explain the period for which a deduction is made.

British Thomson-Houston Co v West (1903)

In some circumstances, a contract may provide that the architect's decision is final as regards certain matters in relation to the building works. In this case, the defendant builders contended that the words of the contract provided that the architect had taken into account all liquidated damages due to be set off or withheld from the sum due to the contractor in the final certificate. Phillimore J rejected this contention. Where the architect's decision was final, the final certificate would constitute a 'strong presumption' that the architect had taken into account liquidated damages.

However, if (as in this case) the contract did not empower the architect to deal with 'penalties' (i.e. liquidated damages), or if it is proved that he had not *in fact* decided the question of liquidated damages, then it will not so bind the employer. Further, in such circumstances, the mere issue of a final certificate certifying the amount due to the contractor would not operate so as to 'estop' the employer for bringing an action to recover liquidated damages.

5.6.4 Extension of time

An employer will not be permitted to recover liquidated damages for the period following the contractual completion date in respect of which an extension of time has been properly granted. The circumstances in which an extension of time may be given are discussed in detail in Chapter 4.

If an extension of time is subsequently granted, any liquidated damages paid or deducted in respect of the period of time which is now subject an extension are repayable to the contractor. Liquidated damages will however be payable in the usual manner if the new completion date is exceeded.

5.6.5 Termination

British Glanzstoff Manufacturing Co Ltd v General Accident, etc, Ltd (1913)

The case before the House of Lords concerned an action between the appellant employer under a building contract and the respondent insurance company, who had guaranteed 'all loss and damage which the appellants might sustain through the failure of the contractors to carry out their contract.' During the works, the contractor ran into financial difficulty and suspended works. The employer engaged third party contractors to complete the works. The question before the House was whether the appellant could recover liquidated damages against the insurer as a result of the delays to completion occasioned by the contractor's suspension and demobilisation. The House held that they could not, stating that upon a proper construction of the contract, the liquidated damages provisions applied only

Liquidated damages

where the contractors had completed the contract and 'did not apply where the control of the contract had passed out of their hands'

Re Yeadon Waterworks Co v Wright (1895)

In this case, the Court of Appeal held that it was permissible in to uphold a special clause that has the effect of keeping the provisions for the payment of liquidated damages alive following a repudiation, even though by that stage the work had been taken out of the hands of the original contractor.

5.6.6 'Waiver'

Clydebank Engineering Co v Yzquierdo y Castaneda (1905)

This case has already been considered above. The employer, having paid the full contract price to the contractor, was held not to have waived his right to recover liquidated damages.

5.6.7 Standard forms

JCT 2005

'Payment or allowance of liquidated damages

2.32.1 Provided:

1 the Architect/Contract Administrator has issued a Non-Completion Certificate for the Works or a Section; and

2 the Employer has informed the Contractor in writing before the date of the Final Certificate that he may require payment of, or may withhold or deduct, liquidate damages,

the Employer may, not later than 5 days before the final date for payment of the debt due under the Final Certificate, give notice in writing to the Contractor in the terms set out in clause 2.32.2.

2 A notice from the Employer under clause 2.32.1 shall state that for the period between the Completion Date and the date of practical completion of the Works or that Section:

1 he requires the Contractor to pay liquidate damages at the rate stated in the Contract Particulars, or less rate stated in the notice, in which event the Employer may recover the same as a debt; and/or

2 that he will withhold or deduct liquidated damages at the rate stated in the Contract Particulars, or at such lesser stated rate, from monies due to the Contractor.*

3 If the Architect/Contract Administrator fixes a later Completion Date for the Works or a Section or such later Completion Date is stated in the Confirmed Acceptance of a Schedule 2 Quotation, the Employer shall pay or repay to the Contractor any amounts recovered, allowed or paid under clause 2.32 for the period up to that later Completion Date.

4 If the Employer in relation to the Works or a Section has informed the Contractor in writing in accordance with clause 2.32.1.2 that he may require payment of, or may withhold or deduct liquidated damages, then, unless the Employer states otherwise in writing, clause 2.32.1.2 shall remain satisfied in relation to the Works or Section, notwithstanding the cancellation of the relevant Non-Completion Certificate and issue of any further Non-Completion Certificate.

Partial Possession by Employer

Contractor's consent

2.33 If at any time or times before the date of issue by the Architect/Contract Administrator of the Practical Completion Certificate or relevant Section Completion Certificate the Employer wishes to take possession of any part or parts of the Works or a Section and the consent of the Contractor has been obtained (which consent shall not be unreasonably delayed or withheld), then, notwithstanding anything expressed or implied elsewhere in this Contract, the Employer may take possession of such part or parts. The Architect/Contract Administrator shall thereupon issue to the Contractor on behalf of the Employer a written statement identifying the part or parts taken into possession and giving the date when the Employer took possession (the 'the Relevant Part' and the 'the Relevant Date' respectively).

* Where the Employer intends to withhold all or any of the liquidated damages payable, either the notice under clause 2.32.2 must comply with the requirements of clause 4.13.4 or 4.15.4 or a separate notice that complies with those requirements must be given.'

Clauses from the JCT Standard Form of Building Contract (2005 edition) by the Joint Contracts Tribunal Limited, Sweet & Maxwell, © The Joint Contracts Tribunal Limited, are reproduced here with permission.

Under clause 2.31 of the *JCT 2005 Standard Form of Building Contract*, the contract administrator is obliged to issue a certificate of non-completion regardless of whether the employer intends to impose liquidated damages: if the employer does, then the issue of a certificate is a precondition to recovering such liquidated damages. However, it seems that, by the wording of clause 2.32.1.2, such a certificate may not be issued after the date of the Final Certificate.

Further, the employer must give written notice requiring the payment of liquidated damages no later than the date of the final certificate. This is a further precondition to the levying of liquidated damages.

As set out above, if the contract administrator fails to properly extend time in accordance with clause 2.28, the employer will be deprived from obtaining liquidated damages for the period in which any such extension should have properly been granted.

It has been suggested that an employer who fails to pay money certified whilst relying on an unfounded right to levy liquidated damages may risk a contractual determination by the contractor under clause 8.9.1.1. (See *Keating on JCT Contracts* at 1.1-113.)

ICE7

'LIQUIDATED DAMAGES FOR DELAY

Liquidated damages for delay in substantial completion of the whole of the Works

47 (1)

(a) Where the whole of the Works is not divided into Sections the Appendix to the Form of Tender shall include a sum which represents the Employer's genuine pre-estimate (expressed per week or per day as the case may be) of the damages likely to be suffered by him if the whole of the Works is not substantially completed within the time prescribed by Clause 43 or by any extension thereof granted under Clause 44 or by any revision thereof agreed under Clause 46(3) as the case may be.

(b) If the Contractor fails to achieve substantial completion of the whole of the Works within the time so prescribed he shall pay to the Employer the said sum for every week or day (as the case may be) which shall elapse between the date on which the prescribed time expired and the date the whole of the Works is substantially completed.

Provided that if any part of the Works is certified as complete pursuant to Clause 48 before the completion of the whole of the Works the said sum shall be reduced by the proportion which the value of the part so completed bears to the value of the whole of the Works.

Liquidated damages for delay in substantial completion where the whole of the Works is divided into Sections.

(2)

(a) Where the Works is divided into Sections (together comprising the whole of the Works) which are required to be completed within particular time as stated in the Appendix to the Form of Tender subclause (1) of this Clause shall not apply and the said Appendix shall include a sum in respect of each Section which represents the Employer's genuine pre-estimate (expressed per week or per day as the case may be) of the damages likely to be suffered by him if that Section is not substantially completed within the time prescribed by Clause 43 or by any extension thereof granted under Clause 44 or by any revision thereof agreed under Clause 46(3) as the case may be.

Liquidated damages

(b) If the Contractor fails to achieve substantial completion of any Section within the time so prescribed he shall pay to the Employer the appropriate stated sum for every week or day (as the case may be) which shall elapse between the date on which the prescribed time expired and the date of substantial completion of that Section.

Provided that if any part of that Section is certified as substantially complete pursuant to Clause 48 before the completion of the whole thereof the appropriate stated sum shall be reduced by the proportion which the value of the part so completed bears to the value of the whole of that Section.

(c) Liquidated damages in respect of two or more Sections may where circumstances so dictate run concurrently.

Damages not a penalty

(3) All sums payable by the Contractor to the Employer pursuant to this Clause shall be paid as liquidated damages for delay and not as a penalty.

Limitation of liquidated damages

(4)

(a) The total amount of liquidated damages in respect of the whole of the Works or any Section thereof shall be limited to the appropriate sum stated in the Appendix to the Form of Tender. If no such limit is stated therein then liquidated damages without limit shall apply.

(b) Should there be omitted from the Appendix to the Form of Tender any sum required to be inserted therein either by subclause (1)(a) or by subclause (2)(a) of this Clause as the case may be or if any such sum is payable to the 'nil' then to that extent damages shall not be payable.

Recovery and reimbursement of liquidated damages

(5) The Employer may:

(a) deduct and retain the amount of any liquidated damages becoming due under the provision of this Clause from any sums due or which become due to the Contractor or

(b) require the Contractor to pay such amount to the Employer forthwith.

If upon a subsequent or final review of the circumstances causing delay the Engineer grants a relevant extension or further extension of time the Employer shall no longer be entitled to liquidated damages in respect of the period of such extension.

Any sum in respect of such period which may already have been recovered under this Clause shall be reimbursed forthwith to the Contractor together with interest compounded monthly at the rate provided for in Clause 60(7) from the date on which such sums were recovered from the Contractor.

Intervention of variations etc.

(6) If after liquidated damages have become payable in respect of any part of the Works the Engineer orders a variation under Clause 51 or adverse physical conditions or artificial obstructions within the meaning of Clause 12 are encountered or any other situation outside the contractor's control arises any of which in the Engineer's opinion results in further delay to that part of the Works

(a) the Engineer shall so notify the Contractor and the Employer in writing and

(b) the Employer's further entitlement to liquidated damages in respect of that part of the Works shall be suspended until the Engineer notifies the Contractor and the Employer in writing that the further delay has come to an end.

Such suspension shall not invalidate any entitlement to liquidated damages which accrued before the period of further delay started to run and subject to any subsequent or final review of the circumstances causing delay any monies already deducted or paid as liquidated damages under the provision of this Clause may be retained by the Employer.'

Liquidated damages

Clauses from the ICE Conditions of Contract (7th edition), published by Thomas Telford and the Institution of Civil Engineers, are reproduced with permission.

Clause 47 of the *ICE* form provides for liquidated damages for the whole of the works, incorporating provisions allowing (amongst other things) a proportional deduction for completed parts and for each section of the works, together with an upper limit of liquidated damages that may be recoverable.

Whilst the wording of clause 47 is a clear attempt to avoid the same being construed as a penalty, this will not oust the court's ultimate jurisdiction to decide this issue (see the cases set out above).

However, the remainder of the clauses provide common-sense, express solutions to some of the problems investigated in the case law set out above. For example, clause 47(4)(a) appears to avoid a conclusion similar to the controversial one in *Temloc v Errill Properties* in case the parties forget to fill in the LAD clause or insert '£nil' against it.

Unlike the position under *JCT*, there is no formal precondition to the deduction or levying of liquidated damages.

NEC3

'Delay Damages X7

X7.1 The Contractor pays delay damages at the rate stated in the Contract Data from the Completion Date for each day until the earlier of

- Completion and
- the date on which the Employer takes over the works.

X7.2 If the completion Date is changed to a later date after delay damages have been paid, the Employer repays the overpayment of damages with interest. Interest is assessed from the date of payment to the date of repayment and the date of repayment is an assessment date.

X7.3 If the Employer takes over a part of the works before Completion, the delay damages are reduced from the date on which the part is taken over. The Project Manager assesses the benefit to the Employer of taking over the part of the works as a proportion of the benefit to the Employer of taking over the whole of the works not previously taken over. The delay damages are reduced in this proportion.'

Clauses from the NEC3 Engineering and Construction Contract are reproduced here with permission from NEC Contracts.

The *NEC3 ECC* contains no default LAD provision. If the same is required, it must be included by way of an 'option'. Option X7 contains no preconditions to the recovery of LADs.

Summary

- The utmost care must be taken when filling in appendices of standard forms: the failure to insert a completion date will prohibit the recovery of LADs; the express inclusion of '£0' or '£nil' against the LAD provision may have even more drastic consequences.
- Depending on the construction of the particular contract in question, the service of notices may be a precondition to the employer's right to recover liquidated damages.
- Care should be taken that the LAD provision selected by the employer is adaptable in the event of sectional completion, if indeed sectional completion is envisaged.
- An extension of time will operate as a total or partial defence to the payment of liquidated damages.
- In general terms, the employer's recovery of liquidated damages from the contractor will cease upon termination of the contract, unless the LAD provision is worded so that it survives such termination.
- It is possible that an employer may waive his rights to claim liquidated damages, but simply paying the contractor the full contract price will not be sufficient to prove this.

6
Loss and expense claims

6.1 INTRODUCTION

The cases in Chapter 2 have illustrated how a contractor may have a claim for additional expenditure arising out of varied or additional work during the course of building works. In addition to chasing payment for such 'extras', a contractor may seek to put in a claim for 'loss and expense'.

A claim for loss and expense is often described as the financial side of a 'delay' claim. However, it does not always follow that delay caused by the employer to a project will occasion loss to the contractor: simply because the contractor has received an extension of time does not always mean he will be entitled to additional payment as well. Moreover, the losses actually suffered will not necessarily be down to the delay: for example, where the progress of the contractor's work is made less efficient as a result of employer actions, the contractor will have a claim for disruption, not delay.

6.1.1 Overriding principles of a loss and expense claim

It is important to recognise that delay and disruption are separate and distinct concepts: delay relates to time, and disruption relates to (in)efficiency and the need for additional resources. Works may be delayed, but not disrupted; conversely, works may be disrupted, but finish to time:

- A 'delay' claim is essentially a claim for prolongation, either of the project or of particular activities. Certain resources (such as project office or management) may have been required for a longer period, or particular activities may have taken longer, so that resources (such as plant or labour) were required for that activity for a longer period, thus incurring additional costs.
- In proving a 'disruption' claim, however, the contractor will have to show that he was obliged to carry out works in

a less efficient manner as a result of acts or defaults of the defendant. There may be periods or areas where the contractor's work was interrupted, or where employer 'events' necessitated the use of additional resources. It goes without saying that disruption claims are more difficult to prove: Not all disruption will trigger the payment of compensation. A contractor will only be entitled to recover such costs if it can prove that the employer prevented or caused hindrance to the execution of the works.

C & P Haulage v Middleton (1983)

A contractor will often be tempted to exaggerate his claim, both in terms of the loss suffered and the extent of any delay. In this particular case, the Court of Appeal indicated that such an approach would be given short shrift:

> 'It is not the function of the courts where there is a breach of contract knowingly to put the plaintiff in a better financial position than if the contract had been properly performed.'

Henry Boot Construction (UK) Ltd v Malmaison Hotel (Manchester) Ltd (1999)

This case has been discussed in the context of concurrent delay, in Chapter 4 above. In that case, Dyson J held that if two delay events occur concurrently, and one of those events entitles the contractor to an extension of time under the contract, the contractor will be entitled to extra time even if the other event is a delay of his own making.

However, the same logic cannot be applied to a loss and expense claim: even though the employer delay may in principle entitle the contractor to recover loss and expense, he will not be able to show that the employer event occasioned such loss, as an event for which he was responsible was occurring at the same time. In other words, where delay is concurrent, a contractor may not be able to show that the additional period on site was brought about by the employer event complained of; he would have suffered the loss on account of his own delay in any event.

As a result, where delay or disruptive events are concurrent, a contractor may obtain an extension of time, but no money.

Loss and expense claims

Summary

- There is a distinction between claims for 'delay' and claims for 'disruption'.
- An exaggerated claim will be fairly transparent to any sensible employer and to the court.
- Where events occasioning loss and expense are 'concurrent', and the contractor is responsible for one of those events, his loss and expense claim may fail.

6.2 CONTRACTUAL FORMALITIES

The established (and arguably most straightforward) route for a contractor to recover loss and expense arising out of delay or disruption to a building contract will be pursuant to the express terms of the contract in question. Such terms ordinarily require the contractor to set out the 'loss and expense' event, together with substantiation of such losses, and the contract administrator or architect will then assess and ascertain if any sums are payable and issue a certificate if so required.

Under the *JCT Standard Form of Building Contract 2005 edition*, the contractor applies for loss and expense under clause 4.23 (clause 26 in the *JCT Standard Form of Building Contract 1980* and *1998* editions), clause 61 under the *NEC3* form and clause 53 under *ICE7*.

Even if an industry-wide standard form is not used, many contracts provide for the service of a timeous notice from the contractor in order to recover loss and expense. This will often be worded as a precondition to contractual relief, and the courts will not shy from enforcing the precondition. However, if the contractor's relief fails under the contract as a result of his failure to comply with formalities, he will nonetheless be entitled to bring a loss and expense claim for breach of contract: in other words, his right to recover will not be lost.

It is possible, however, that express words of the contract could restrict the contractor's remedy at common law if notice provisions are not complied with.

Strachan & Henshaw Ltd v Stein Industrie (UK) Ltd and GEC Alsthom Ltd (1997)

This decision of the Court of Appeal concerned an appeal from an arbitration arising out of works carried out under a subcontract relating to the construction of a combined cycle gas turbine power station in Cambridgeshire. The contract contained, at clause 44.4, what is sometimes referred to as an 'exclusive remedy' clause:

> 'The Purchaser and the Contractor intend that their respective rights, obligations and liabilities as provided for in the Conditions shall be exhaustive of the rights, obligations and liabilities of each of them to the other arising out of, under or in connection with the Contract or the Works, whether such rights, obligations and liabilities arise in respect or in consequence of a breach of contract or of statutory duty or a tortious or negligent act or omission which gives rise to a remedy at common law. Accordingly, except as expressly provided for in the Conditions, neither party shall be obligated or liable to the other in respect of any damages or losses suffered by the other which arise out of, under or in connection with the Contract or the Works, whether by reason or in consequence of any breach of contract or of statutory duty or tortious or negligent act or omission.'

The Court of Appeal held that if the parties wished to limit their potential liability to one another as so provided by clause 44.4, there was no reason why the law should prevent them, even if it rendered 'worthless' an action in damages for breach of a contractual right.

It is submitted, however, that a tribunal will construe a clause which gives a contractor the right to claim for losses caused by any particular breach (e.g. a loss and expense clause) broadly where it is the contractor's exclusive remedy. Whilst such a clause could include conditions precedent to recovery, a Tribunal may be slower to give effect to such a construction in the face of an exclusive remedy clause unless the wording of the agreement allows no other outcome.

Loss and expense claims

Summary

- A notice may be a precondition to the bringing of a loss and expense claim under a construction contract.
- A contractor should supply any notice in close in time as possible to the event occasioning him loss and expense, and substantiate the same in as much detail as is possible.
- Although it will depend on the terms of the contract, the right to a claim under the contract will not normally shut out the contractor's alternative claim in damages for breach.

6.3 STANDARD FORMS

6.3.1 JCT 2005

'Loss and Expense

Matters materially affecting regular progress

4.23 If in the execution of this Contract the Contractor incurs or is likely to incur direct loss and/or expense for which he would not be reimbursed by a payment under any other provision in these Conditions due to a deferment of giving possession of the site or relevant part of it under clause 2.5 or because the regular progress of the Works or of any part of them has been or is likely to be materially affected by any of the Relevant Matters, the Contractor may make written application to the Architect/Contract Administrator. If the Contractor makes such application, save where these Conditions provide that there shall be no addition to the Contract Sum or otherwise exclude the operation of this clause, then, if and as soon as the Architect/Contract Administrator is of the opinion that the regular progress has been or is likely to be materially affected as stated in the application or that direct loss and/or expense has been or is likely to be incurred due to such deferment, the Architect/Contract Administrator shall from time to time thereafter ascertain, or instruct the Quantity

Surveyor to ascertain, the amount of the loss and/or expense which has been or is being incurred; provided always that the Contractor shall:

1 make his application as soon as it has become, or should reasonably have become, apparent to him that the regular progress has been or is likely to be affect;

2 in support of his application submit to the Architect/Contract Administrator upon request such information as should reasonably enable the Architect/Contract Administrator to form an opinion; and

3 upon request submit to the Architect/Contract Administrator or to the Quantity Surveyor such details of the loss and/or expense as are reasonably necessary for such ascertainment.

Relevant Matters

4.24 The following are the Relevant Matters:

1 Variations (excluding any loss and/or expense relating to a Confirmed Acceptance of a Schedule 2 Quotation but including any other matters or instructions which under these Conditions are to be treated as, or as requiring, a Variation);

2 Instructions of the Architect/Contract Administrator:

1 under clause 3.15 or 3.16 (excluding an instruction for expenditure of a Provisional Sum for defined work);

2 for the opening up for inspection or testing of any work, materials or goods under clause 3.17 (including making good), unless the cost is provided for in the Contract Bills or unless the inspection or test shows that the work, materials or goods are not in accordance with this Contract; or

3 in relation to any discrepancy in or divergence between the Contract Drawings, the Contract Bills and/or other documents referred to in clause 2.15;

Loss and expense claims

3 suspension by the Contractor under clause 4.14 of the performance of his obligations under this Contract, provided the suspension was not frivolous or vexatious;

4 the execution of work for which an Approximate Quantity is not a reasonably accurate forecast of the quantity of work required;

5 any impediment, prevention or default, whether by act or omission, by the Employer, the Architect/Contract Administrator, the Quantity Surveyor or any of the Employer's Persons, except to the extent caused or contributed to by any default, whether by act or omission, of the Contractor or of any of the Contractor's Persons.'

Clauses from the JCT Standard Form of Building Contract (2005 edition) by the Joint Contracts Tribunal Limited, Sweet & Maxwell, © The Joint Contracts Tribunal Limited, are reproduced here with permission.

The contractor's application for payment in respect of variations is covered by the 2005 form at clauses 5.6-5.9; payment in respect of overheads and profit may well have been allowed for in the contractor's variation claim and the contractor must be careful not to make the same application twice as this will amount to double recovery.

Absent a notice, the contractor cannot claim under clause 4.23. However, an application for an extension of time under clause 2.28 will not be a precondition to a loss and expense claim under 4.23. (See *Fairweather v Wandsworth* (1987) 39 BLR 106.)

London Borough of Merton v Leach (1985)

This case has been discussed in Chapter 4 above. The Court held that in relation to the parallel provision in the 1963 standard form, applications for loss and expense:

- should be clear and as precise as needs be to allow the architect to carry out his proper duties as contract administrator, i.e. to form a competent opinion as to whether or not the contractor is entitled to relief;

- should be submitted within a reasonable period;
- did not prevent a contractor for bringing an alternative claim for loss and expense by way of damages. However, this may not be the case if the contract has been amended so as to include an exclusive remedy clause (see *Strachan & Henshaw v Stein* (above)), or where damages are claimed as a result of concurrent delay. See *Henry Boot v Malmaison* (below).

Rees & Kirby v Swansea City Council (1985)

This case is discussed in more detail below. It is thought to be authority for the proposition that if a contractor claims finance charges as part of his loss and expense claim, his application ought to state that he has suffered loss and expense as a result of being kept out of his money.

6.3.2 NEC3

Loss and expense will be awarded to the contractor under the *NEC3* if he can prove that a 'compensation event' (broadly speaking, an event which does not arise from the contractor's fault) will occasion him loss. As set out above in Chapter 4, clause 61.3 contains an important 'time-barring' provision: should the contractor fail to notify a compensation event within eight weeks of becoming aware of that event, he will not recover relief either in the form of time or money, unless the Project Manager should have notified the Contractor of the event but did not.

6.3.3 ICE7

'Additional payments

53 (1) If the Contractor intends to claim a higher rate or price than one notified to him by the Engineer pursuant to sub-clauses (3) and (4) of Clause 52 or Clause 56(2) the Contractor shall within 28 days after such notification give notice in writing of his intention to the Engineer.

(2) If the Contractor intends to claim any additional payment pursuant to any Clause of these Conditions other than sub-clauses (3) and (4) of Clause 52 or Clause 56(2) he shall give notice in writing of his intention to the Engineer as soon

Loss and expense claims

as may be reasonable and in any event within 28 days after the happening of the events giving rise to the claim.

Upon the happening of such events the Contractor shall keep such contemporary records as may reasonably be necessary to support any claim he may subsequently wish to make.

(3) Without necessarily admitting the Employer's liability the Engineer may upon receipt of a notice under this Clause instruct the Contractor to keep such contemporary records or further contemporary records as the case may be as are reasonable and may be material to the claim of which notice has been given and the Contractor shall keep such records.

The Contractor shall permit the Engineer to inspect all records kept pursuant to Clause 53 and shall supply him with copies thereof as and when the Engineer shall so instruct.

(4) After giving of a notice to the Engineer under this Clause the Contractor shall as soon as is reasonable in all the circumstances send to the Engineer a first interim account giving full and detailed particulars of the amount claimed to that date and the grounds upon which the claim is based.

Thereafter at such intervals as the Engineer may reasonably require the Contractor shall send to the Engineer further up to date accounts giving the accumulated total of the claim and any further grounds upon which it is based.

(5) If the Contractor fails to comply with any of the provisions of this Clause in respect of any claim which he shall seek to make then the Contractor shall be entitled to payment in respect thereof only to the extent that the Engineer has not been prevented from or substantially prejudiced by such failure in investigating the said claim.

(6) The Contractor shall be entitled to have included in any interim payment certified by the Engineer pursuant to Clause 60 such amount in respect of any claim as the Engineer may consider due to the Contractor provided that the Contractor shall have supplied sufficient particulars to enable the Engineer to determine the amount due.

If such particulars are insufficient to substantive the whole of the claim the Contractor shall be entitled to payment in respect of such part of the claim as the particulars may substantiate to the satisfaction of the Engineer.'

Clauses from the ICE Conditions of Contract (7th edition), published by Thomas Telford and the Institution of Civil Engineers, are reproduced with permission.

Clause 53 of *ICE7* deals with 'additional payments' under this particular standard form. The important provisions to note are clauses 53(5) and 53(6), which deal with the contractor's failure to comply with the formalities of clause 53.

6.4 HEADS OF LOSS

There is little authority on what heads of loss may be claimed as part of a contractor's loss and expense claim. This is because such claims rely broadly upon first principles; provided that the contractor can show that an act or omission for which the employer is responsible caused the loss complained of, and that the loss complained of is not too remote, then the contractor will recover. The cases below examine some of the most common heads of loss claimed by a contractor on 'loss and expense' grounds.

6.4.1 Prolongation costs

'Prolongation costs' is the shorthand term applied to the costs of additional on- and off-site overheads occasioned by delay to construction works. These are conceptually distinct from disruption costs (as to which, see below). They may include 'fluctuations', allowing the contractor to recover increases in the cost of machinery, materials or labour as a result of delay.

6.4.2 Increased site overheads

In short, this head of loss relates to additional labour, utilities, and plant that is required on site for a longer period than the contract anticipated as a result of a delay to the completion date.

Shore v Horwitz Construction Co Ltd v Franki of Canada Ltd (1964)

This decision of the Canadian Supreme Court concerned a dispute with the defendant subcontractor for the driving of piles in relation to the construction of a government building. The piles were defective and the defendant had to carry out the works again. The claimant main contractor sought to recover damages in relation to additional overheads and the cost of idle plant during the four months that the project was in delay. The Supreme Court held that overheads were indeed recoverable, but hiring charges were only recoverable if the contractor did not own the plant; if it does, it should be treated as a non-profit-making asset (see *Whittal Builders* (below)). (It is noteworthy that Judson J dissented, on the basis that the main contractor could not prove that it could have moved onto another job in the mean time. This appears to be a precondition to recovery: see *JF Finnegan* (below).)

Whittall Builders v Chester-le-Street DC (1985)

The defendant was a district council that employed the claimant contractor to carry out various works to houses which were to be made available for the contractor's access in lots of 18 at a time. The handover of houses fell into disarray, with the result that houses were released late and in an inefficient sequence. By November 1974, the council began to accelerate and no further problems with possession occurred. The contractor claimed (amongst other things) the loss of productivity of plant on site during the course of the works.

The Court found that maintenance and depreciation costs of retaining its plant at site would be recoverable, as it was 'highly probable' that the resources could have been used elsewhere.

Alfred McAlpine Homes North Ltd v Property and Land Contractors Ltd (1995)

This dispute arose out of the construction of houses by the defendant in Shipton, Yorkshire. The claimant issued a notice under clause 23 of the *JCT Standard Form of Building Contract* to postpone the contractor's works. The defendant duly submitted a loss and expense claim under clause 26 of the contract for additional preliminary costs, comprising overheads and profit and idle plant on site. The claimant refused to agree this claim. On appeal from an arbitrator's award, the Court held (amongst other things) that:

- Under the terms of the contract, the contract administrator was obliged to 'ascertain' – i.e. 'make certain' the cost claimed, and a general assessment would not be permissible.
- A claim for hire charges for idle plant was recoverable in principle, but the contractor must demonstrate his actual loss; a reference to reasonable hire charges is not sufficient.

6.4.3 Increased office overheads

As all contractors are engaged in running a business, they will have overheads as a matter of course. However, delays or disruption to works may mean that the contractor is precluded from diverting such overheads to new projects (which themselves would contribute to those overheads), or even that the costs of running the contractor's general business increase, such as through the employment of additional staff.

Sunley (B) & Co Ltd v Cunard White Star Ltd (1940)

The defendant agreed to transport a tractor and a scraper owned by the claimant and required for the carrying out of groundworks in the Channel Islands. The defendants literally missed the boat as a result of their failure to provide proper appropriate and timely transportation to deliver the plant to port. The claimants were deprived of the use of the plant for one week. The Court of Appeal held that the claimant was entitled to recover damages reflecting the depreciation in the value of the machinery and maintenance costs for the period in which it lay idle.

Whittall Builders v Chester-le-Street DC (1985)

The contractor claimed (amongst other things) the cost of off-site overheads and profit arising from the prolonged and unproductive use of machinery and labour on site. The Court held, following *Bernard Sunley*, that if evidence pointed to alternative profit-earning work being available, overheads would be recoverable.

JF Finnegan Ltd v Sheffield City Council (1988)

The defendant council instructed the claimant contractor to carry out refurbishment work to houses under the *JCT Standard Form of Building Contract 1963 edition*. The claimants brought a claim for loss and expense as a result of its inability to adhere to the contractual timetable resulting from batches of houses being handed over out of sequence. The Court held that the contractor's loss in respect of lost overheads and profit (as to which see below) was to be calculated by looking at the fair annual average of the contractor's overheads and profit as a percentage figure, multiplied by the contract sum and the period of weeks of delay, divided by the contract period (this is known as the 'Hudson formula'). However, recovery of such costs is only possible if the contractor can demonstrate that he could have been employed on another contract that would have the effect of funding the overheads during the period of delay.

Alfred McAlpine Homes North Ltd v Property and Land Contractors Ltd (1995)

This case has been discussed above. The Court ruled that if the company in question is a single contract company, it is entitled to recover its fixed overheads expenditure as a result of delay. If the company had several projects, then its loss would be the shortfall in the contribution to such overheads that the volume of work was expected to make (i.e. it can recover its 'unabsorbed overheads').

6.4.4 Increase in cost of materials

Sometimes delay to a building project will mean the contractor is hit in the pocket when delays to a project impinge upon the procurement process, and the cost of materials rises during that period of delay. The editors of *Keating on Construction Contracts* (8th edition) at 8-055 submit that such costs are recoverable as damages and can either be proved by reference to actual loss, or published inflation indices. However, the contract in question will often contain provisions for 'fluctuations'.

Peak v McKinney (1970)

This case has been discussed in some detail in various contexts in Chapters 4 and 5 above. In this case it was also held that a liquidated damages provision will encompass any sums which would be payable to the contractor pursuant to a fluctuations clause under the contract.

Summary

- The terms of the contract should be the first port of call in investigating a contractor's entitlement to recover the cost of increased preliminaries or for 'fluctuations', and the basis upon which the same may be calculated.
- The increased cost of preliminaries occasioned by delays to the works is a legitimate head of loss. In order to recover, the contractor must generally prove that he could have obtained profitable work in the period of delay that would have funded the overheads in that period.
- If the contractor owns machinery, he may recover depreciation and maintenance costs; if the machinery is hired, then he may recover any extra hire charges.
- In principle, the increased cost of off-site overheads will be recoverable if it can be shown that there was profitable work available that such overheads could have been turned to.
- It has been suggested (see *Keating on Construction Contracts* (8th edition, 2006) at 8-050) that, in the absence of a contractual clause setting out a rate for preliminary charges in the event of delay, a contractor should be cautious in adopting a simple 'percentage uplift' approach. He should look to establish his proper loss in the normal manner. This is consistent with the reasoning in *Tate & Lyle* (as to which, see below).

Loss and expense claims

6.4.5 Wasted management time

Sometimes particular employees or senior management will be engaged in dealing with a project for substantially longer than a contractor may have anticipated at the time of tendering. Where management time has been spent in dealing with the consequences of events causing delay or disruption for which the employer is responsible, a contractor may seek to be compensated for the same by the employer.

Tate & Lyle v GLC (1982)

The defendant authority entered into a contract to construct two new piers for the Woolwich ferry in East London in close proximity to the claimant's business premises. Prior to the building works, riparian access was provided to the business premises by barge moorings, which were rendered unusable as a result of heavy silt deposits occasioned by the two new piers. The claimants alleged that they had spent considerable time from both a management and supervisory perspective in dealing with the defendant's failure to dredge away the silt deposits. The claimants sought to recover such costs from the defendant. Forbes J held that there was evidence that managerial time was spent on dealing with remedial measures and rearranging berthing schedules to enable the delivery of sugar, and that the same could properly form the head of special damage. However, he went on to warn that such a head of loss was 'extremely difficult to quantify' and, in the absence of timesheets or written records, no recovery was permissible. Forbes J declined to 'follow Admiralty practice and award a percentage on the damages', stating that to do so would be 'pure speculation'.

Babcock Energy Ltd v Lodge Sturtevant Ltd (1994)

The claimant had contracted to provide boilers and ancillary equipment necessary for a power station. The claimant in turn subcontracted with the defendant for the provision of two electrostatic precipitators. Subsequently, it emerged that the electrostatic precipitators provided by the defendant did not meet the contract specifications. The claimant duly compensated the employer, and sought to recover the same sum from the defendant.

One of the heads of loss claimed related to the management time spent by the claimant in investigating the claim. The defendant submitted that no sum could be recovered in respect of this item because the staff costs were fixed and would have been incurred in any event: it was the cost of taking on additional agency staff which represented the true measure of loss. The Court rejected this argument, holding that it was sufficient to show (as the claimant had shown) that time was spent by permanent staff in dealing with the defendant's breach. The amount of time so spent was also a valid measure of loss.

Try Build Ltd v Invicta Tennis Ltd (2000)

In this case concerning the construction of tennis halls in Southampton, HHJ Bowsher QC hinted that management time losses would be recoverable, even if the assessment exercise is somewhat hypothetical:

> 'where the time of a senior manager has been taken up by extra duties made necessary by the wrongdoing of a defendant, the employer…has lost the benefit of that individual's time which ought to have been devoted to his ordinary duties even (or perhaps especially) if the time lost was time which might have been spent looking out of the window thinking. The value of that time lost to the company may be enormous or small, but it can only be assessed by reason of the cost of the employee to the company. Where I have felt that the claim for management time is inadequately proved, I have for the most part taken the defendants' estimate, appreciating that this may well be substantially less than the actual cost which might have been shown if records were kept. I am not criticising anyone for not keeping records of management time, but their absence leads to difficulties of proof.'

Phee Farrar Jones Ltd v Connaught Mason Ltd (2003)

The claimant was a leaseholder of commercial premises in Charing Cross, London. The defendant contractor was responsible for flooding during refurbishment works to the premises. The flooding caused considerable damage, and during the course of the requisite remedial works, the claimant relocated its staff to alternative office accommodation. The claimant claimed the cost of 90 hours of wasted management time spent by a senior employee in organising the move to alternative accommodation. HHJ Toulmin QC refused to allow the claim, holding that:

> 'Managerial expenses can be claimed as damages if it is established that the claimant's trading was disturbed in a way which led to a discrete expense being incurred (e.g. overtime) or by a specific loss of revenue, which would otherwise have been obtained. There is no evidence that this happened. In particular, there is no evidence that income-generating opportunities were lost in the course of Mr Chandler organising the move to Alfred Place.'

Riverside Property Investments v Blackhawk Automotive (2004)

In this case, HHJ Coulson QC affirmed the position that a claimant could recover damages for their managerial and supervisory expenses provided that such expenses were directly attributable to the defendant's default. However, in the circumstances, as in *Tate & Lyle*, the claim failed because the plaintiffs had kept no records of the time expended and the claim could not therefore be quantified.

Aerospace Publishing Ltd v Thames Water Utilities Ltd (2007)

In this case, a mains water pipe for which the defendant was responsible ruptured, leading to the flooding of the claimant's premises and to the damage of various rare publications archived therein. The defendant admitted liability, but the issue of quantum was appealed when the first instance judge failed to give adequate reasons for his assessment.

Amongst other items, it was considered whether the defendant was liable for the staff costs incurred by the claimant in relation to, and consequent on, the flood. Lord Justice Wilson identified the following propositions which applied where such costs were claimed:

> '(a) The fact and, if so, the extent of the diversion of staff time have to be properly established and, if in that regard evidence which it would have been reasonable for the

claimant to adduce is not adduced, he is at risk of a finding that they have not been established.

(b) The claimant also has to establish that the diversion caused significant disruption to its business.

(c) Even though it may well be that strictly the claim should be cast in terms of a loss of revenue attributable to he diversion of staff time, nevertheless in the ordinary case, and unless the defendant can establish the contrary, it is reasonable for the court to infer from the disruption that, had their time not been thus diverted, staff would have applied it to activities which would, directly or indirectly, have generated revenue for the claimant in an amount at least equal to the costs if employing them during that time.'

Bridge UK.Com Ltd v Abbey Pynford plc (2007)

The defendant contracted to construct the foundations to the claimant's premises, which were to be of sufficient strength to support a printing press weighing 62 tonnes. As a result of various defects in the floor, the defendant's works were not completed in time. The claimant claimed its costs and losses incurred as a result of this delay, amongst which was a claim for £7,680.00 as management time incurred in dealing with the problems caused by the defendant's defective performance.

The Court confirmed that the retrospective assessment of the management time spent represented a valid method of calculation, agreeing that in the absence of records, evidence in the form of an assessment made from memory was acceptable. However, Ramsay J noted that such an estimate was necessarily approximate, and thus applied a discount of 20 per cent to the sum claimed to allow for its inherent uncertainty. He also reiterated the importance of showing that the time lost would have otherwise generated revenue for the claimant.

Summary

- The expenditure of additional managerial time is, in principle, recoverable, provided that the party can prove

that such expenses were caused by genuine disruption to its trading routine as a result of a breach.
- A 'percentage-based' approach is likely to fail. The party seeking to recover such losses must prove his actual losses suffered, ideally through making proper references to any available timesheets.

6.4.6 Disruption costs

Loss of productivity/uneconomic working

This head of loss is conceptually different from prolongation costs. There may be no delay at all, yet the contractor nevertheless incurs costs as a result of inefficient deployment of labour or plant. If the contractor can show that the planned and actual use of labour and plant differed, and this difference can be tied into an employer event (such as late changes imposed to the construction programme or prevention of access to particular parts of site), he can recover the costs occasioned by working at a different time or in a different sequence.

Whittall Builders v Chester-le-Street DC (1985)

This case has been discussed above. During the course of the works, the claimant had to keep resources on site in the event that possession of further houses was made available. The Court awarded damages to the claimant and held that the correct way to measure unproductive work was by comparing the value of work achieved per man prior to November 1974 with the amount paid to each man thereafter (when the works were not disrupted). On the facts, it was found that one-third of the sums paid to the contractor were recoverable as inefficient labour costs.

Tate & Lyle v GLC (1982)

This case is discussed above. It is probable that a 'percentage-based' approach will also not suffice to prove a disruption claim.

6.4.7 Loss of profit

If delay or disruption leads to a diminution in the contractor's turnover, he may be able to claim loss of profit, provided that he can show that he would have used the lost turnover profitably. (See *Keating on Construction Contracts* (8th edition, 2006) at 8-052.)

Sunley (B) & Co Ltd v Cunard White Star Ltd (1940)

This facts of this case are set out above. In addition to the depreciation claim, the contractor claimed loss of profit, but was unable on the facts to prove that he had lost any profit on the Channel Islands contract as a result of the week-long delay in the delivery of the plant.

6.4.8 Finance charges

FG Minter Ltd v WHTSO (1980)

The claimant contractors were employed to construct a teaching hospital in Wales under the *RIBA Standard Form of Building Contract 1963 edition*. The claimant borrowed heavily to fund the project. At trial it was established that the defendant was responsible for the late or non-issue of instructions, drawings, details and levels, and the claimant brought a claim for loss and expense including, amongst other things, a claim to recover finance charges for the periods in which plant and machinery lay idle as a result of the delays. The Court of Appeal held that such charges could legitimately be recovered as part of a party's 'direct loss and expense' under the contract.

Rees & Kirby v Swansea City Council (1985)

Delays of approximately one year were caused to the building of a housing estate in Swansea by the claimant contractors. Some of the delay at least was attributed towards the negotiation of an 'ex gratia' settlement in respect of the claimant's loss and expense claims and a proposal that the basis of the fixed-price contract be modified so as to accommodate fluctuations negotiations. The Court of Appeal confirmed that finance charges were a recoverable head of loss, but where loss and expense is attributable delay caused

Loss and expense claims

by an independent (i.e. non-employer) event (such as the aforementioned negotiations), finance charges would not be recoverable for that period.

6.4.9 Loss of bonus

Some contracts (either from their inception or through a subsequent variation during the works) provide for the payment of a 'bonus' should timely or early completion be achieved, in order to incentivise swift, efficient progress on site. There may be circumstances where the contractor complains that his recovery of the bonus payment was scuppered as a result of employer events causing delay.

Bywaters & Son v Curnick & Co (1905)

This case concerned refurbishment works carried out to the defendant's restaurant in 1903. The contract, agreed in early 1903, provided for a bonus payment of £360 if the works were completed within nine weeks. The progress of the works was held up by a party wall dispute with the adjoining property, with the result that possession was not granted until May 1903, and the defendants refused to pay the bonus. The Court of Appeal held that the party wall dispute constituted an act of prevention and that the bonus payment was recoverable.

John Barker Construction Ltd v London Portman Hotel Ltd (1996)

The defendants were hoteliers who engaged the claimant contractors to carry out refurbishment works to the Portman Hotel in London, pursuant to a *JCT Standard Form of Building Contract, 1980 edition*. Different floors were subject to different completion dates, with the final floors to be completed by August 1994. Delays occurred for which the defendants appreciated the contractors were entitled to an extension of time. An agreement was reached between the parties in June 1994 whereby the claimants waived their right to an extension of time in return for entering into an acceleration agreement, whereby they would be paid a bonus of £90,000 if they could complete by August 2004. Further delays occurred, occasioned by the issue of architect's instructions. Practical completion occurred in September 1994. The contractor obtained an extension of time covering part of the additional time, but not all. The Court held that the hoteliers had prevented the contractors from achieving timely completion and that they were entitled to be paid 50 per cent of the bonus payment, as a result of the claimant's 'loss of a chance' of recovering the same. It appears that the full amount was not payable because the judge recognised that there were 'all manner of [other] reasons' why the contractor may have failed to complete by August 2004.

Summary

- The recovery of a bonus payment is payable in principle as damages.
- Whether or not the full amount be payable depends on the strength of the contractor's evidence that he would have completed by the bonus date.
- Recovery will be prevented if ensuing delays are the fault of the contractor.

6.4.10 Sums paid in settlement of third party claims

There are many situations in which the contractor will find himself acting as a 'middleman' during a building project. The most obvious will be in his position as a party to contracts with the employer (above him) and subcontractor (below him). It frequently occurs that delay and disruption to the contractor's works caused by employer events will also affect the works carried out by one of those subcontractors. In such circumstances, the subcontractor (not being privy to the main contract) may bring a claim against the contractor, and the contractor will often seek to reach a commercial settlement of any such claim. The cases below investigate when sums paid under such settlements are recoverable.

Biggin & Co Ltd v Permanite Ltd (1951)

The claimants were purchasers of goods from the defendants for re-sale to the Dutch government. The goods were defective, and arbitration proceedings brought by the Dutch government were settled by the claimants. The claimants sought to recover the sums paid under the settlement agreement from the defendants. The trial judge held that the settlement was irrelevant. The Court of Appeal disagreed:

> 'I think that the learned judge ... was wrong in regarding the settlement as wholly irrelevant. I think, though it is not conclusive, the fact that it is admittedly an upper limit would lead one to the conclusion that, if reasonable, it should be taken as the measure. The result of the learned judge's conclusion is that the plaintiff must prove his damages strictly and must show that they equal or exceed £43,000. If that involves, as it would here, a very complicated and expensive enquiry, still that has to be done. The law, in my opinion, encourages reasonable settlements, particularly where, as here, strict proof would be a very expensive matter. The question in my opinion is: What evidence is necessary to establish reasonableness? I think it relevant to prove that the settlement was made under legal advice ... The plaintiff must, I think, lead evidence ... as to what would probably be proved if ... the arbitration had proceeded, so that the court can come to a conclusion whether the sum paid was reasonable. The defendant may ... seek to show that it was not reasonable ... He might in some cases show that some vital matter had been overlooked' (per Somervell LJ).

The plaintiffs must establish a prima facie case that the settlement was a reasonable one' (per Singleton LJ).

Oxford University Press v John Stedman Group (1990)

The first defendant was a firm of architects engaged by the claimants in relation to the design and construction of a warehouse. The main contractor was joined into the proceedings by the architects. Following completion of the warehouse, cracking and crazing occurred to the floor. During trial, the parties reached a settlement. The main contractor also settled with a subcontractor who had laid the floor of the warehouse. The proceedings continued between the defendants, following which the judge held that the responsibility for the cracking and crazing was to be apportioned on a 60/40 and a 50/50 basis respectively between the defendant and the main contractor. In order to recover against the main contractor, the Court held that the first defendant had to establish that its settlement was reasonable with the claimant, but did not have to prove strictly the claims made against it in all respects.

Bovis Lend Lease v RD Fire Protection (2003)

This case concerned fire protection and dry lining works in relation to the construction of a shopping centre in Glasgow pursuant to a *JCT Standard Form of Building Contract With Contractor's Design, 1981 edition*. The main contract was between the claimant developer and Braehead Glasgow Ltd, and the contract sum was substantial, in excess of £180m. Disputes over the payment of loss and expense and the leyving of liquidated damages occurred between Braehead and the claimant, which were the subject of a settlement agreement in January 2002. The developer sought to recover part of the sums paid out under the settlement agreement from the defendant, who had carried out a small proportion of the fire protection works.

In reviewing the authorities, HHJ Thornton QC deduced the following conclusions from *Biggin v Permanite* and subsequent cases:

- The *Biggin v Permanite* principles apply if a claim is for an indemnity or for breach of contract, and whether or not liability was admitted under a settlement agreement.
- The rationale behind those principles is that a defendant will be taken to have foreseen that liability to a third party might arise out of his breach of contract, and that the liability may lead to compromise.
- The settlement figure paid to compromise the third party claim represents the upper limit of what may be recovered from a defendant. Any sum in excess of this would represent a profit to the claimant The *Biggin v Permanite* principles are principles of evidence as well as rules concerning the quantification of damages. even if the claimant decided to prove its claim in the usual manner as opposed to relying on a settlement, the settlement would operate as a 'ceiling'.
- The claimant need only prove that his settlement was reasonable, without establishing in detail the extent and quantum of the third party claim.

Loss and expense claims

- Expert or professional evidence which the claimant took into account in deciding to compromise the third party claim may be adduced to establish reasonableness.
- Breach on the part of the defendant must be established, as well as the causal link between the defendant's breaches and the claimant's breaches towards the third party.
- If the amount paid under the settlement was unreasonable, it would provide no evidential foundation to establish the claimant's loss. However, it would still operate as a 'ceiling' to limit recovery.
- The tribunal must establish what part of an overall settlement of a multi-party or multi-issue dispute is attributable to the relevant breaches of contract of each defendant.

CFW v Cowlin (2006)

The facts of this case are set out in Chapter 5 above. The contractors sought to recover sums which it had paid out to the employer under a settlement agreement relating to liquidated damages levied by the employer for late completion of the works. HHJ Thornton, having found that the LAD clause was not penal and thus properly enforceable, permitted recovery on the grounds that the settlement was reasonable, even though the LAD provision was capable of operating harshly against the contractor. It would therefore seem that a 'harsh' settlement may nonetheless amount to a reasonable settlement.

John F Hunt v ASME Engineering Ltd (2007)

The claimant was a subcontractor responsible for the demolition of commercial premises, in turn appointing the defendant to construct a temporary steel structure to support the building's facades while the demolition works were carried out. In the course of construction, sparks from the welding work set light to weather-proofing materials on the facades, which caught fire. The claimant settled the main contractor's claim, seeking to recover these sums from the defendant. The defendant resisted the claim on the grounds that the claimant was not liable to the employer in tort, as had been alleged.

Having found that the claimant had no liability to the employer, a key issue was whether the settlement was necessarily unreasonable, entailing a discussion of the scope of the principle in *Biggin & Co Ltd v Permanite Ltd*, on the basis of which settlement claims are passed on. The Court determined that the absence of liability did not of itself render the settlement unreasonable, but that what was reasonable was a question of fact to be resolved in all the circumstances of the case.

Summary

- In principle, sums expended in settlement of third party claims (including claims arising out of delay or disruption) constitute a recoverable head of loss.
- Whether or not the claimant has taken legal advice with regard to the settlement will be a material consideration in judging whether or not the settlement was reasonable.
- When arriving at a settlement (especially if that settlement relates to multiple claims), a contractor should take care to allocate particular sums to particular losses or liabilities.

6.4.11 Cost of claim collation

Preparing a claim, whether in adjudication, arbitration or litigation, is not a task to be undertaken lightly. Often the process will take considerably longer and cost considerably more than the project team could have reasonably envisaged at the start of the dispute. Contractors and employers alike may allocate a sizeable chunk of their own resources or staff to the preparation of a claim. A successful party will generally look to the discretion of the tribunal to recover his legal costs. However, different principles apply when it comes to considering whether the costs of 'claims collation' are recoverable. This can broadly be split into two categories, viz. 'expert assistance' and the party's 'own costs', which are explored below.

Loss and expense claims

Expert assistance

Manakee v Brattle (1970)

The defendant was the builder of a cesspool which was defective. The claimant duly instructed a surveyor to prepare plans and a specification for a replacement, and issued a writ for the cost of carrying out such works. The claimant omitted to claim the costs of obtaining the report in its damages claim. Moccata J nontheless awarded the same as costs. He further held that it such costs were 'expenditure that could have been claimed as damages' as the evidence of the surveyor was 'vital, and included the preparation, before the issue of the writ, of plans and specification in order to obtain quotations'. (This was also the conclusion of the Court in *Peak v McKinney*.)

Bolton v Mahadeva (1972)

The claimant installed a hot water system at the defendant's property. The defendant alleged that the same was faulty, and obtained an expert report which backed up his allegations. The Court of Appeal held that the costs of procuring an expert report would not be recoverable as damages:

> 'So far as the defendant's claim in respect of fees for the report which he obtained from his expert is concerned, it seems to me quite clear that that report was obtained in view of a dispute which had arisen and with a view to being used in evidence if proceedings did become necessary, and in the hope that it would assist in the settlement of the dispute without proceedings being started. In those circumstances, I think that the judge was right in reaching the conclusion that that report was something the fees for which, if recoverable at all, would be recoverable only under an order for costs.' Per Cairns LJ.

George Fisher Holding Ltd v Multi Design Consultants (1998)

The claimant brought proceedings against the defendant in respect of various roof defects following the construction of a warehouse by the defendant. Costs were incurred by the claimant in the expert preparation of a remedial scheme (the

'Sarnafil' scheme) which was ultimately held by the Court to be inappropriate. However, such costs were also incurred in preparing for the trial of the action by providing a necessary foundation for the claimant's case that the Sarnafil scheme was appropriate. The Court held that, in principle, such costs could be recoverable as damages (i.e. as part of the remedial scheme) and as costs in the litigation: in other words, had the Sarnafil scheme been appropriate, the claimant would have (in theory at least) had a choice.

See the case of *James Longley v South West Regional Health Authority* (1983) 25 BLR 56 for a case involving the recovery of costs paid out to claims consultants.

Party's own costs

The London Scottish Benefit Society v Chorley (1884)

In this case, the Court of Appeal was confronted by a litigant in person who was himself a solicitor. There it was held that he was entitled on taxation to the same costs as if he had employed a solicitor, except in respect of items which the fact of his acting directly rendered unnecessary. Brett MR reasoned that:

- When an ordinary litigant comes to court, he may recover as costs his solicitor's fees but nothing for his own loss of time.
- If a solicitor who represented himself was not entitled to ordinary costs for his own time, he would have no incentive to argue the case himself. A route which might enable a reduction in the costs of a claim would thereby be closed off.

Therefore 'it would be absurd to permit a solicitor to charge for the same work when it is done by another solicitor, and not to permit him to charge for it when it is done by his own clerk.'

The decision lends support, as noted in *Sisu Capital Fund Ltd v Tucker & Ors*, to the principle that a litigant in person who has some professional skill can recover in respect of the time spent exercising that skill.

Loss and expense claims

For recent judicial comment on this case, see *Malkinson v Trimm* [2002] EWCA Civ 1273.

Re Nossen's Letter Patent (1969)

Costs were incurred on research and experimentation in defending an application for patent infringement, with part of the work being carried out by the defendant's own experts on the defendant's own premises. Lloyd-Jacob J held that if expert assistance was required in the case of litigation by a corporation, it may well be that the corporation's own employees are the most suitable experts to employ and that the direct costs should be recoverable. Although *The London Scottish Benefit Society v Chorley* was not expressly mentioned, the decision is clearly consistent with *Re Nossen's Letter Patent*.

Buckland v Watts [1970] 1 QB 27

Here, the position of a litigant in person who had claimed for his time in researching the law but who was not himself a solicitor was not entitled to claim costs accrued in preparing his case. The Court rooted its decision in *The London Scottish Benefit Society v Chorley* to reiterate that a professional solicitor should only be able to recover any costs in respect of work which would usually be done by a professionally qualified solicitor. A non-solicitor could not recover in respect of his own legal research. (Note that a litigant in person may recover generally for his (legal) work done on his case, although CPR 48.6 places an absolute cap on the amount recoverable (namely two thirds of the sum which would have been allowed if the litigant in person had been represented by a legal representative). The litigant in person can recover for the same categories of costs and disbursements which would have been allowed if the work had been done, or the disbursements made, by a legal representative on the litigant's behalf. The onus is on the litigant in person to prove financial loss in respect of any item of work, failing which the amount recoverable is fixed by statutory instrument (currently £9.25 per hour).) A further proposition was advanced by Sir Gordon Willmer, who suggested that professionals might only recover something in respect of their own skill in so far as they qualified as witnesses. This is clearly inconsistent with *Re Nossen's Letter Patent*.

Richards & Wallington (Plant Hire) Ltd v A Monk & Co Ltd (1984)

The claimant contractor's claim was formulated by a non-executive director and by a claims consultant. Bingham J rejected the claim to have the cost of their work included, pointing out that the work was non-expert in nature, being a simple factual exercise. Accordingly 'they were certainly not independent experts' and did not fall within the *Re Nossen's Letter Patent* exception. Costs of this nature (i.e. linked to non-expert fact-gathering) fell 'within the ordinary costs that a litigant must bear of digging out his own factual material, through his own employees, to prove his own case.'

Admiral Management Services Ltd v Para-Protect Ltd (2002)

This decision, which pre-dated *AMEC Process* and *Energy Ltd v Stork Engineers & Contractors BV (No 4)* by just ten days, provides a helpful synthesis of the pre-*AMEC* case law. Here, the claimant suspected that the defendant was wrongfully using its confidential information, to which end an order was obtained for the removal of documents and floppy disks. The claimant's employees were engaged in examining the material. The Court reasoned that:

- The general rule is that the work of a party's employees in investigating, formulating and prosecuting a claim does not qualify for an order for costs.
- Re Nossen's Letter Patent was an exception to this rule in that a corporate litigant could recover the costs of expert services provided by its own staff.
- The accepted position in *Re Nossen's Letter Patent* was to be preferred to Sir Gordon Willmer's judgment in *Buckland v Watts*.
- *Richards & Wallington (Plant Hire) Ltd v A Monk & Co Ltd* showed how narrow the exception was: to be recoverable, the work done by a litigant's staff had to be of an expert nature, and not simply of a fact-finding character.

Loss and expense claims

- For the *Nossen* exception to apply, the staff concerned must have a sufficient level of experience to qualify as experts and the nature of the work must qualify for a costs order.
- Familiarity with a party's business does not make a witness an expert for the purposes of the recovery of costs.

AMEC Process and Energy Ltd v Stork Engineers & Contractors BV (No. 4) (1996)

In this claim relating to the laying of steel pipes in the North Sea oil fields, the claimant had engaged its own personnel to carry out much of the work involved in the collection and analysis of primary evidence. They also undertook much of the preparation of visual aids on behalf of the expert. HHJ Thornton QC held that:

- Cases such as *Re Nossen's Letter Patent* which pre-dated the CPR had little or no bearing on the interpretation and application of the CPR costs code.
- The time charges involved in employing the claimant's personnel came within the definition of 'fees, charges, disbursements, expenses, remunerations' for the purposes of CPR 43.2(1)(a).
- It would be contrary to the overriding objective if necessary expense which was incurred at a lower cost than if the claimant's solicitors' employees had undertaken the work was not recoverable.

Sisu Capital Fund Ltd v Tucker & others (2006)

In this case, a number of office-holders engaged in the administration of a company had spent a considerable period of time addressing an application to have them removed from their position. Again, the question before the Court was whether a litigant must bear the costs of digging out his own factual material through his own employees. The office-holders argued that:

- The *London Scottish Benefit Society* case has a wide application because a solicitor litigant in person recovers for his time. Therefore other professional litigants in

person should recover for their time, regardless of whether they are using their professional skills.
- If a professional can charge for his own time, so too should he be able to charge for the time of his staff.
- *AMEC* shows that the CPR mark a shift in the approach of the courts.

Having reviewed the relevant case law, Warren J rejected the office-holders' submissions, finding that *The London Scottish Benefit Society* case was limited in scope to litigants in person who are also solicitors. By extension, a litigant in person who is a professional could only recover for the costs of his services if they were used to address issues which would normally require expert attention. The position of an office-holder was no different: the fact that an office-holder may have to bring or defend litigation as part of his duties did not mean that it was part of his profession to do so. It was the nature of the work done and the nature of the workers' expertise which were crucial. The decision in *AMEC* was also carefully dismantled, with Warren J stating that *Re Nossen's Letter Patent* cannot just be dismissed as having no bearing on the CPR costs code.

HHJ Thornton QC said that as a matter of construction, the time charges fell within the definition of 'costs', but gave no reason for their doing so and did not consider the earlier, relevant case law.

The *AMEC* decision, if applied, would extend the range of recoverable costs and make litigation more expensive.

Summary

- Whether the cost of expert assistance will be recoverable as a head of damages or as costs in the litigation will generally depend on whether such assistance was requested for the purposes of considering the breach, or for the purpose of the proceedings (i.e. either bringing or defending a claim).
- The position in respect of a litigant's 'own costs' is less certain. However, it is suggested that the *Sisu* approach is the more likely to be followed (as indeed it has been in *Societa Finanziara Industriche Turistiche SpA v di Balsorano*

Loss and expense claims

& *Ors* (unreported, 30 June 2006)) because of its consistency with previous authority and because HHJ Thornton QC's view that the CPR were a watershed for the purposes of this issue is probably an oversimplification.

6.4.12 Other losses

Whether an employer is responsible for losses arising out of more unusual circumstances resulting from delay and/or disruption (that are not discussed above) will depend on the extent of the employer's knowledge at the time of contracting.

6.5 GLOBAL CLAIMS

Often it will be very difficult for a contractor to attribute particular losses to particular periods of delay or disruption events. In such circumstances, the delay or disruption claim may be presented on a 'global basis' – sometimes going little further than preparing a somewhat rude comparison between the 'planned' and the 'as-built' construction programmes. Traditionally these were the subject of strike-out applications (such as in *Wharf Properties*), although given the development of the law it is unlikely that such an application will succeed save in the most extreme cases. 'Global' claims are frequently also referred to as 'total loss' claims or 'rolled up' claims.

Wharf Properties v Eric Cumine Associates (No. 2) (1991)

The clients' actions against their architects for negligent design and contract administration were struck out as incomplete and therefore disclosing no reasonable course of action. Per Lord Oliver:

> 'the pleading is hopelessly embarrassing as it stands . . . .. in cases where the full extent of extra costs incurred through delay depend upon a complex interaction between the consequences of various events, so that it may be difficult to make an accurate apportionment of the total extra costs, it may be proper for an arbitrator to make individual financial awards in respect of claims which can conveniently be dealt with in isolation and a supplementary award in respect of the financial consequences of the remainder as a composite whole. This

has, however, no bearing upon the obligation of a plaintiff to plead his case with such particularity as is sufficient to alert the opposite party to the case which is going to be made against him at the trial.'

Since *Wharf Properties* and prior to the decision of the Scottish Inner House of Session in *John Doyle* (as to which, see below), there has been a considerable amount of case law on the topic of 'global claims' (*J Crosby & Son v Portland UTC* (1967) 5 BLR 121; *Merton LBC v Stanley Hugh Leach Ltd* (1985) 32 BLR 51; *Mid-Glamorgan County Council v J Devonald Williams & Partner* [1992] 29 Con LR 129; *McAlpine Humberoak v McDermott International* (1992) 52 BLR 1; *ICI v Bovis Construction Ltd* [1993] Con LR 90; *British Airways Pensions Trustees Ltd v Sir Robert McAlpine & Sons Ltd* (1994) 72 BLR 26; *John Holland Construction & Engineering Pty Ltd v Kvaerner RJ Brown Pty Ltd* (1996) 82 BLR 83; *Bernhard's Rugby Landscapes Ltd v Stockley Park Consortium Ltd* (1997) 82 BLR 39; *AMEC Process & Energy Ltd v Stork Engineers & Contractors BV* [2000] BLR 70; *John Holland Property Ltd v Hunter Valley Earth Moving* [2003] Const. LJ 171). Space does not permit an in-depth analysis of all of these cases, although some of the more pertinent principles arising from them are briefly set out below.

John Holland Construction and Engineering Pty Ltd v Kvaerner RJ Brown Pty Ltd (1996)

Pursuing a 'global claim' will only be permissible in cases where it is impractical to disentangle specific losses which are attributable to specific causative events.

Bernhard's Rugby Landscapes Ltd v Stockely Park Consortium Ltd (1997)

A party must set out its case with 'sufficient particularity', and state the nexus of causation/interaction of events with adequate clarity. Whilst a claimant may of course plead its claim on liability or quantum as it sees fit, the defendant is entitled to know what case it has to meet. 'Sufficient particularity' is a matter of fact and degree in each case; a balance must be struck between excessive particularity and basic information.

Laing Management (Scotland) Ltd v John Doyle Construction Ltd (Scotland) (2004)

John Doyle was engaged by Laing to carry out certain work packages for the construction of new headquarters for Scottish Widows, pursuant to an amended form of *Scottish Works Contract*. In the litigation, John Doyle sought an extension of time of some 22 weeks, together with a substantial claim for loss and expense (over £4m). The loss and expense claim was calculated on a classic 'global' basis, by comparing pre-contract estimates and actual costs.

Although the claim in *John Doyle* was for loss and expense, it is submitted that the principles are of equal application to a claim for delay. The following principles can be extracted from the judgment of the Inner House:

- A contractor must normally plead and prove individual causal links between each alleged breach or claim event and each particular delay for a delay claim under a construction contract to succeed.
- If the consequences of each of the alleged delay events cannot be separated, and if the contractor is able to demonstrate that the fault for all of the events on which he relies is the employer's, it is not necessary for him to demonstrate causal links between individual events and particular heads of loss.
- However, if a significant cause of the (cumulative) delay alleged was a matter for which the employer is not responsible, the contractor's global claim will fail.
- There may be a delay event or events for which the employer is not responsible. Nonetheless, provided that these are insignificant, an apportionment exercise may be carried out by the tribunal.
- Pursuing a 'global claim' will not be permitted if it is advanced in lieu of proper pleading. The fundamental requirements of any pleading must be satisfied, namely:
  - that fair notice must be given to the other party of the facts relied upon together with the legal consequences that are said to flow from such facts;
  - so far as causal links are concerned, in a global claim situation there will usually be no need to do more than set out the general proposition that such links

exist (causation being largely a matter of inference from expert's reports); and
- heads of loss should be set out comprehensively.

Great Eastern Hotel Company Ltd v John Laing Construction (2005)

In this case, the defendants advanced the argument that the claimant's case ought to fail as it was unable to demonstrate the causal nexus between major breaches of contract and particular loss and damage. HHJ Wilcox ruled:

> 'I am satisfied that the Trade Contractor accounts are global claims, and if such a claim is to succeed, GEH must eliminate from the causes of the loss and expense element all matters which are not the responsibility of Laing. That requirement is mitigated in this case, because it was not possible to identify a causal link between particular events for which Laing was responsible, and the individual items of loss. Such an analysis was approved by the Court of Session Inner House in *John Doyle Construction Limited v Laing Management (Scotland) Limited* … I am satisfied … that the dominant cause of Trade Contractor delay was in fact the delay to the project caused by Laing's proven breaches.'

London Underground Limited v Citylink Telecommunications Limited (2007)

The defendant consortium contracted to replace the entire communications systems throughout London's underground rail network, together with the continued operation of that system. The replacement works were carried out, but were considerably delayed. The various delay claims were settled by an Arbitrator's award. In making the award, the Arbitrator had indicated that he was following the process in relation to global claims advised by Lord Macfadyen in *Laing Management (Scotland) v John Doyle Construction Ltd*. This requires a causal link to be established between delay events and periods of delay except where it is impossible to do so, in which case a global claim may succeed (but only if the dominant cause of delay is attributable to the defendant).

Loss and expense claims

Ramsay J, in considering the claimant's case that the Arbitrator determined the claim based on a case which was neither pleaded nor addressed in evidence, reviewed the courts' approach to global claims. He accepted the approach set out in *Laing v Doyle*, stating that in global claims there will be a need for the tribunal to analyse the evidence to determine if causation may be established. In such cases, neither party will have a specific opportunity to deal with a case based on the tribunal's particular findings. In short:

> 'Tribunals frequently have to deal with cases where a claim or a defence has not wholly succeeded and it is necessary to determine what result flows from the partial success or failure. Provided that the result is based on primary facts which have been in issue in the proceedings, there can in principal be no objection to a tribunal taking such a course.'

6.6 THE SCL PROTOCOL

In October 2002 the Society of Construction Law published a *Delay and Disruption Protocol* in an attempt to foster a transparent, balanced and unified approach to the management of delay and disruption issues as and when they arise. It is not intended to be a statement of law, or indeed to take precedence over the express terms of a contract; rather, it represents a scheme for dealing with delay and disruption issues that is fair and viable.

In relation to concurrent delay, the *Protocol* provides that where 'Contractor Delay to Completion' has effect concurrently with 'Employer Delay to Completion', the existence of the former should not reduce any extension of time due. This appears to reflect the logic adopted in *Malmaison* (see above and Chapter 4).

The *Protocol* frowns upon a 'wait-and-see' approach to questions of delay. Its core objective is to encourage parties to deal with applications for an extension of time as close in time as possible to the delay event, rather than waiting for its full effect to be felt and then analysed afterwards.

Prolongation costs will only be recoverable by the contractor to the extent that such costs can properly be attributable to

183

employer delay events rather than his own. The evaluation of any sum due is made by reference to the period when the effect of the employer risk event was felt, not by reference to the extended period after completion of the works.

The *Protocol* also encourages early completion, with appropriate contractual machinery to deal with problems which may emerge should the employer prevent the contractor from finishing the works prior to the agreed contractual completion date. Should a contractor intend to finish early, then such an intention ought to be communicated to the employer at the time of contracting.

The *Protocol* discourages the making of global claims, on the basis that the same is 'rarely accepted by the Courts'. Guidance is provided as to the keeping of records to prevent such a course of action, and emphasis placed on setting out details of the employer events relied upon so that the defendant may know with sufficient particularity the case that is being made against it.

It is submitted that the *Protocol*'s assertion very probably overstates the position and, as matters currently stand, particularly following the decision in *John Doyle*, it is probably incorrect.

6.7 EXPERT DELAY/DISRUPTION EVIDENCE

6.7.1 Delay claims

The primary focus of expert evidence in claims involving delay and disruption will be on delay. As technology progresses, and as disputes become more and more complicated, such experts often place heavy reliance on computer programs or simulations to carry out delay 'modelling'. Over the years, there have been a number of judicial pronouncements as to the necessity or desirability of software-based critical path analysis as evidence to support a delay claim.

John Barker Construction Ltd v London Portman Hotel Ltd (1996)

An architect's impressionistic (rather than calculated) assessment was 'fundamentally flawed' because, amongst other things, he 'did not carry out a logical analysis in a methodical way.' The case was taken by many as a ringing endorsement of software based critical path analysis methods.

Royal Brompton Hospital NHS Trust v Hammond (No. 7) (2001)

His Honour Judge Richard Seymour QC appeared to approve the adoption of an impressionistic approach. The Judge appeared to approve the following view (at p. 176):

> '... the making of assessments of whether a contractor was entitled to an extension of time ... did not depend upon any sort of scientific evaluation of any particular type of material, but simply upon impression formed on the basis of previous experience.'

Skanska Construction UK Ltd v Egger (Baronry) Ltd (2004)

In this case, HHJ Wilcox QC criticised what was presented as a very sophisticated 'impact analysis' by stating that the results gleaned from such an analysis were 'only as good as the data put in'. He went on to criticise the computer project as 'complex' and 'rushed', and held that the Court could have no confidence in its accuracy.

Great Eastern Hotel Company Ltd v John Laing Construction Ltd (2005)

This case has been considered above in the context of 'global' claims. A further decision of HHJ Wilcox QC, the Court again lambasted a computerised critical path analysis program as the same was based on milestone dates which did not exist, and had simply been identified retrospectively once the project was completed.

6.7.2 Disruption claims

Activity-specific claims

The activity-specific claim represents the most traditional approach to a disruption claim. It involves identifying either a single activity or a limited group of activities. The exercise is then to compare the actual costs attributable to undertaking those activities with the hypothetical cost which those activities would have involved but for the effect of the disruption. The observations in the *John Doyle* case cited above (section 6.5) lend some support to this approach.

'Measured mile' claims

The Society of Construction Law's *Delay and Disruption Protocol (2002)* lends support to this approach, which has an established successful track record in international civil engineering claims. The *Protocol* guidance puts the matter as follows:

> 'The most appropriate way to establish disruption is to apply a technique known as the "Measured Mile". This compares the productivity achieved on an un-impacted [undisrupted] part of the Contract with that achieved on the impacted [disrupted] part. Such a comparison factors out issues concerning unrealistic programmes and inefficient working. The comparison can be made on the man-hours expenses or the units of work performed. However care must be exercised to compare like with like. For example, it would not be correct to compare work carried out in the learning curve part of an operation with work executed after that period.'

However, where the works in question are not comprised of a high volume of broadly similar and repetitive work, there may be more difficulty in harnessing this technique. Thus, it may be of limited application for claims arising out of conventional building work.

Summary

- A programme-based delay analysis is no substitute for examining the facts in the usual manner, i.e. through

Loss and expense claims

witness evidence and scrutinising contemporaneous documentation, such as site diaries.

- Assumptions made in the construction of retrospective computer analyses are controversial: the claimant who relies on the same runs the risk that the program will not be accepted by the tribunal for the purposes for which it was created.
- Computer models are expensive and susceptible to criticism over their cost. If both parties have experts, it is prudent for both to meet for the purposes of agreeing what is the most appropriate software package for them to use and what is to be done with it.
- In all cases, the expert must be fully conversant with the facts, the chronology and the links between the different activities on the critical path.
- Where there are realistic alternatives, the expert should address them. Thus, there should be a discussion of alternative events and alternative time slices, where appropriate. Equally, there will be cases in which an alternative presentation can be deployed. Such a presentation may represent a true alternative or may be used as a cross-check.
- It is essential that the product is subjected to a continuous 'reality check'. A simple presentation of 'as-planned' as against 'as-built' can be deployed as a cross-check for a more sophisticated analysis.

7
Termination

A contract may be terminated in accordance with its terms and there may then be mechanisms set out for determining what sums might be payable from one party to another. A contract may be terminated by one party accepting the repudiatory breach of contract of another. The termination of a contract will often be contentious; and if the legitimacy of the termination is itself is in dispute this can and will give rise to potential claims for damages. This chapter summarises the key cases which have dealt with issues arising out of the termination of contracts, and the interrelationship between contractual termination and common law repudiation.

7.1 CONTRACTUAL TERMINATION

It is important that a party follows the procedure laid down in the contract carefully if the termination is to be considered valid.

7.1.1 Compliance with notice provisions

Hounslow LBC v Twickenham Garden Developments (1971)

For a period of six months, the relevant construction site was closed by a strike. A number of months after work resumed, the architect purported to give notice to the contractors that they had failed to proceed regularly and diligently with the works, and that unless within 14 days there was an appreciable improvement, the council would be entitled to determine their employment. Some weeks later, the council purported to determine the contractors' employment under the contract. The contractors informed the council that their actions were regarded as repudiatory, but that they would not accept the repudiation of the contract, and that they elected to proceed with the contract works in accordance with the terms of the contract.

The council sought to restrain the contractors until judgment in the action or further order from 'entering, remaining or otherwise trespassing on the site or from interfering in any way with the council's lawful possession of the same'.

The Court held that on the facts, the council fell short of establishing the factual basis that underlay the notice. However, as to the validity of the form of the notice, the Court considered that a notice of default by the architect under clause 25(1) of the *RIBA conditions* was required to direct the contractor's mind to what is said to be amiss. The conditions did not requiring the architect, at his peril, to spell out accurately in his notice further and better particulars of the particular default in question. If the contractor had sought particulars of the alleged default and had been refused them, other considerations might have arisen.

Architectural Installation Services v James Gibbons Windows (1989)

The defendants gave by letter to the claimants notice that they required the claimants to comply with a particular condition of the contract and work the full working day required by that condition. A 'follow-up' to that letter was said to be a purported notice of termination issued some 11 months later, referring to the withdrawal of labour from the site.

The first letter was considered to be a valid 'first' notice despite the fact that it did not refer to the termination machinery itself or to the consequences of non-compliance. However, it was held that where a contract provides for termination of the contract by a warning notice followed by a termination notice, and two notices have been served, a party can only rely on that provision if an ordinary commercial businessman can see that there is a sensible connection between the two notices both in content and in time.

In this case, there was no sensible connection in terms of either content or time.

Tara Civil Engineering Ltd v Moorfield Developments Ltd (1989)

The claimants were contractors for roadworks, employed under the *ICE Conditions 5th edition*. The engineer served a notice on the claimant condemning certain works, and thereafter issued a certificate pursuant to clause 63(c) of the contract conditions (the equivalent of clause 65(1)(h) in the *ICE 7th edition*). This permitted a termination notice to be served following the contractor's failure to remove or pull down and replace goods or materials, having already received a notice condemning the same. After this notice was served, the defendant employer then notified the claimant of its intention to expel it from the site. The claimant obtained an *ex parte* injunction preventing its removal from the site. There followed an application to discharge the injunction. The claimant argued that clause 63 of *ICE 5th edition* had to be read in conjunction with clause 39, which provided the engineer with powers to order in writing the removal from site of non-compliant materials. The Court held that clause 63 can and should be construed without any suggestion that it was limited by clause 39 or that it should be preceded by a notice which is in some way identifiably referable to clause 39. The engineer and the employers have various options open to them under the contract, and those options should not be restricted.

Wiltshier Construction (South) Ltd v Parkers Developments Ltd (1996)

The claimants were employed as management contractors for the defendants pursuant to the *JCT Standard Form of Management Contract (1987 edition)*. The defendants alleged default on the claimants' part 'to carry out the works with due diligence and in an economical and expeditious manner', and purported to operate the contractual machinery to determine the contract. An injunction to prevent determination was sought. The Court held that the notice was invalid because (1) it was not the function of the claimant to carry out 'the works'; (2) the claimants were not under a contractual duty to ensure that the project was carried out in an economical and expeditious manner; (3) the notice did not indicate, even in general terms, what was amiss with the claimants' performance (as opposed to the contractors' performance); (4) the notice purported to put the burden on the claimants to provide information as to why an unstated complaint should not be considered accurate: it was not the purpose of a termination notice to seek to obtain an explanation from the claimant as to cost and time overruns on the project; and (5) the claimants were given no indication of what he was supposed to do within 14 days by way of proceeding regularly and diligently with the work. The cost and time overruns of themselves could not be cured in that time.

Ellis Tylin Ltd v Co-operative Retail Services Ltd (1999)

The defendant contracted with the claimant to provide the maintenance and repair services for a period of three years with provision for revision of rates of payment at the end of the first and second years. The contract was operated for a year. The relationship between the parties did not run smoothly. The contractual right of the claimant to terminate the agreement only arose if they first made a written proposal for the alteration of future fees. The written proposal was to be made after the expiry of ten months from the commencement of the contract. The commercial purpose shown by the clause was considered to be that the parties should be free to negotiate for variation of the fee effective from the first and second anniversaries of the contract, and if negotiations are unsuccessful, either party should be at liberty to terminate, in the case of the claimant by giving notice effective not earlier than three months after the anniversary. The claimant was not entitled to give a notice at a date or in terms calculated to produce a termination of the contract earlier than allowed for by the clause or otherwise produce a result inconsistent with this purpose. However, notices may be valid if they are 'sufficiently clear and unambiguous to leave a reasonable recipient in no reasonable doubt as to how and when they are intended to operate'. In particular, the Court considered that a party in the position of defendant might wish to insist on receiving the whole of the three months notice, because to receive any less would deprive them of a valuable right to have their equipment serviced. The Court rejected the suggestion that the parties to the agreement can have intended that the notice given should be not a day more than three months.

Hadley Design Associates Ltd v The Lord Mayor and Citizens of the City of Westminster (2003)

The defendant local authority engaged the claimant surveyor to provide professional services in respect of an estate in Pimlico pursuant to a contract that referred to the terms of the *RICS Conditions of Engagement for Building Surveying Services (1981 edition)*. In 1996, the defendant issued a one-month termination notice pursuant to the RICS terms and conditions. The claimant claimed that the termination of the contract was wrongful and entitled it to damages representing the profit which it would have made had it been permitted to complete all of the work which would have been involved in providing the services required under the contract in respect of all the repairs necessary to any block of flats on the estate. It was argued that in a contract of this nature, there was an implied term that a termination could not be served other than for good cause. This was rejected on the basis that, amongst other things, it gave rise to very serious considerations of policy where it was suggested that one party to a contract should be compelled to receive services from another from whom he no longer wishes to receive them when the contract between the parties contains a mechanism for determination by notice, which mechanism has been operated. The Court held, in the circumstances of the case, that the one month notice period for termination was reasonable, if and insofar as that was a valid consideration at all in considering the legitimacy of the termination notice.

Robin Ellis Ltd v Vinexsa International Ltd (2003)

A contract had come into being after lengthy pre-contractual negotiation incorporating the *JCT IFC 84* form of contract. The *IFC 84* standard form determination procedure involves the participation of the architect at the first stage and the employer at the second stage where there has been a default. The architect has a discretion whether or not to issue the first default notice and must exercise that discretion without any interference from the employer and the employer has a discretion, not to be exercised unreasonably or vexatiously, whether or not to issue the second determination notice which can only be exercised if the default has not been corrected for 14 days after service of the default notice and only then if the discretion is exercised within ten days after the expiry of the first 14 days.

The claimant removed its labour from the site. In response, the architect issued a default notice under clause 7.2.1 informing the claimant that the defendant had without reasonable cause wholly suspended the carrying out of, and had failed to proceed regularly and diligently with, the works in that it had insufficient operatives on site at the relevant times. This notice was the first of two notices envisaged by the default and determination clause 7 of *JCT IFC 84*. Labour returned to site, but was then withdrawn again. The architect therefore issued a second default notice. This notice was then withdrawn, but quite independently on the same day the claimant's solicitors sent a notice stating that if the defendant did not return to site within five days, then it would determining the defendant's employment. The defendant did not return and the employment was terminated pursuant to clause 7.2.3.

The Court considered that the general rule of construction applicable to determination clauses is that they, and the procedure for determination they provide for, should be construed and applied strictly.

It was held that once a clause 7.2.1 default notice has been served in relation to a specified default, no further default notice can be served if and when it is repeated. However, since the second clause 7.2.1 notice was invalid and had, in any case been withdrawn and since, as found by the arbitrator, the claimant had defaulted in the specified manner and had then repeated that default, the claimant was entitled to serve the determination notice pursuant to clause 7.2.3.

7.1.2 Unreasonable or vexatious termination

The following four cases have all considered the common requirement in standard terms which prevents one party from using the contractual machinery for termination 'unreasonably or vexatiously'.

J M Hill v London Borough of Camden (1980)

An interim certificate for £84,518 was issued but that amount was not paid promptly by the defendant employer. The claimant contractors therefore reduced their labour and plant at the site. The defendants then wrote to the claimants alleging that they had failed to proceed 'regularly and diligently' with the works and treating this as repudiatory breach of conduct. The claimant sent by recorded delivery a letter to the defendant notifying them pursuant to clause 26(1)(a) of the 1963 *JCT Standard Form* that unless they received payment within seven days they would serve notice of determination of their employment 'which shall be effected forthwith upon the service'.

Seven days later the claimant wrote to the employers a further letter determining their employment. Pursuant to the contract terms, the right to terminate could not be exercised 'unreasonably or vexatiously'. It was held by the Court that it had not been unreasonable for the claimant to determine its employment since it had good reason for taking advantage of the remedies given to it by the contract. Lord Justice Ormrod considered:

> 'But what the word 'unreasonably' means in this context, one does not know. I imagine that it is meant to protect an employee who is a day out of time in payment, or whose cheque is in the post, or perhaps because the bank has closed, or there has been a delay in clearing the cheque, or something -something accidental or purely incidental so that the Court could see that the contractor was taking advantage of the other side in circumstances in which, from a business point of view, it would be totally unfair and almost smacking of sharp practice.'

Lubenham Fidelities & Investments Company Ltd v South Pembrokeshire District Council (1983)

In considering the phrase 'unreasonably or vexatiously' within termination clauses, the Court considered that construction contracts often extended over long periods of time and involved the use of considerable resources in land and materials, and that if they are not completed the financial and other consequences can be very serious. The inclusion of provisos in standard forms of contract were intended, in the judgment of HHJ Newey QC, to prevent parties from standing on their legal rights when the effect of their doing so will be quite disproportionate to their grounds of complaint. 'Unreasonably' in a proviso relates principally to lack of proportion. The Court also considered that 'vexatiously' must mean something different from 'unreasonably', and imports an intention to harass or distress.

John Jarvis v Rockdale Housing Association (1986)

In a building project governed by the *JCT Standard Form of Building Contract (1980 edition)*, a nominated subcontractor withdrew from site having started late and leaving its piling work defective and incomplete. The architect instructed the claimant contractor to postpone the works pursuant to clause 23.2 of the conditions. After one month had expired the claimant gave notice purporting to terminate their employment under the contract, pursuant to clause 28.1.3.4 which provided that if the carrying out of the whole or substantially the whole of the works were suspended for a period of one month by reason of architect's instructions issued under clause 23.2 'unless caused by some negligence or default of the contractor' then the contractor could by notice determine its employment under the contract, provided that the notice was not given 'unreasonably or vexatiously'.

In considering the latter phrase, the Court considered that the right test was whether a reasonable contractor, in the same circumstances as was the relevant contractor at the time when he gave the notice, would have thought that it was unreasonable or vexatious to give such a notice. 'Vexatious' was considered to mean 'an ulterior motive to oppress harass or annoy'.

Reinwood Ltd v L Brown & Sons (2007)

The defendant contractor left the site having purported to determine the contract under clause 28.2.4 of the *JCT Standard Form 1998*, on the basis that the claimant employer had failing to pay a sum due under an interim certificate, and thereby had repeated a specified default under clause 28.1.1.1. The notice was served seven days after the money had been due, and the money was in fact paid the day after the notice was served. The claimant claimed that the delay in payment had been caused by an administrative error. Six months earlier, there had been one previous default by the claimant, in relation to which the defendant had served an initial notice of default.

Having found the notices to be valid, the Court held that it was for the claimant to show that the contractor had determined the contract unreasonably or vexatiously, that latter term meaning with the motive being to oppress, harass or annoy the employer. This was an objective test, in that the fact that the individual contractor may have thought that his conduct in determining the contract was reasonable is not conclusive. The answer was to be ascertained by reference to the acts of a reasonable contractor, given all the circumstances which could include having regard to the contractor's own commercial interests, and whether the determination would have a disproportionate effect on the employer.

The circumstances considered by the Court included the fact that delay in payment had been caused by the claimant's own failure or incompetence, difficulties the defendant had experienced with a special purpose vehicle similar to the claimant company within the same group on another contract, and the manner in which the defendant's claims for loss and expense, allowed in earlier valuations, were then being valued downwards or disallowed in their entirety. The Court held that the defendant had acted neither vexatiously nor unreasonably.

7.1.3 Contractual termination and other existing rights

The express reservation of rights preserves the normal rights of common law.

Architectural Installation Services v James Gibbons Windows (1989)

See above for facts. Following the invalidity of the formal termination notice, the question arose as to whether the common law rights of termination remained. The Court saw no reason for any implication of any term to the effect that the termination provision was to be the only machinery for terminating the contract, to the exclusion of common law rights of termination. Reliance upon the absence of words such as, 'without prejudice to other rights and remedies' was rejected. The Court considered that construction contracts were already sufficiently complicated when the draftsmen seek to state what they do mean.; they should not be burdened with the additional task of stating what they do not mean. See, however, *Lockland Builders*, below.

Lockland Builders Ltd v John Kim Rickwood (1995)

Clause 2 of the contract between developer and contractor provided a procedure by which the developer could terminate the contract should he be dissatisfied with the rate of progress, or the quality of materials or workmanship. The clause was not expressed to be 'without prejudice to any other rights or remedies' or similar. It was held that clause 2 impliedly precluded the developer from terminating the contract otherwise than by the exercise of his rights under clause 2, since the complaints made fell squarely within the scope of clause 2, i.e. complaints as to the quality of materials and workmanship. However, it was considered that clause 2 would not have done so in relation to breaches outside the ambit of clause 2, e.g. by the contractor walking off the site when the works were still substantially incomplete.

Laing & Morrison Knudsen v Aegon (1997)

LMK, as contractor, entered into a subcontract with a mechanical works supplier. The subcontractor provided a bond. The subcontractor ran into financial difficulties before completing the works. LMK gave notice of termination, and LML requested payment from the defendant bondsman. Clause 20, the termination provision within the contract, was expressed to be without prejudice to any other legal or equitable right or remedy. The question arose whether LMK could, having terminated the subcontract works at a time when the subcontractor was in repudiatory breach of the subcontract, recover the additional cost of completing the subcontract works under the bond. This depended, in part, upon whether the act of terminating the contract in purported pursuance of clause 20, was itself an affirmation of the contract such that LMK could not longer rely upon the repudiatory breaches. The Court held that an election to affirm the contract or to accept the repudiation must be clear and unequivocal. The letter of termination pursuant to clause 20 was not an election not to repudiate the contract and therefore an affirmation of it because clause 20 under which the right was purported to be exercised was expressed to be without prejudice to any other legal or equitable right or remedy. In this case, it was also material that the ground for termination was the appointment of an administrative receiver, and not therefore a ground that of itself was repudiatory in nature.

Dalkia Utilities Services Plc v Celtech International Ltd (2006)

A contract for the provision of services over 15 years contained a clause, upon which the claimant relied to terminate the agreement, which stated: 'In the event of the CLIENT being in material breach of its obligations to pay the CHARGES the COMPANY shall have the right to terminate this Agreement immediately.' It was held that as at the date of the claimant's valid termination letter, the defendant was in material breach of its obligation to pay the charges. The question arose whether the letter of termination could have amounted to acceptance of a common law repudiatory breach and thus a different basis for determining the sums payable from one party to the other.

The Court held that an innocent party can exercise either his contractual or his common law right of termination, or, prima facie, both. He is not disentitled to rely on the common law on the ground that recourse to a contractual right constitutes an affirmation of the contract since in both cases he is electing to terminate the contract for the future (i.e. to bring to an end the primary obligations of the parties remaining unperformed) in accordance with rights that are either given to him expressly by contract or arise in his favour by implication of law. However, the Court concluded it does not follow that in all cases a contractual notice will amount to an acceptance of a repudiatory breach. If the notice makes explicit reference to a particular contractual clause, and nothing else, that may, in context, show that the giver of the notice was not intending to accept the repudiation and was only relying on the contractual clause; for instance if the claim made under the notice of termination is inconsistent with, and not simply less than, that which arises on acceptance of a repudiation. On the facts, in light of the markedly different consequences that would follow from the contractual or common law determination, the notice was construed as taking effect in, and only in, accordance with the express terms of the contract.

7.2 REPUDIATORY BREACH OF CONTRACT

Hoenig v Isaacs (1952)

The claimant sued for the price of his work consisting of the decoration and furnishing of the defendant's flat. The defendant sought to avoid payment of the balance owing (some 40 per cent of the contract price) on account of defects in the furniture which nevertheless he was using. The Court held that a breach consisting of negligent omission or bad workmanship where the work was substantially completed is not sufficient to constitute repudiatory breach of a lump sum contract. The claimant was entitled to the balance, less the cost of making good such defects as the defendant was able to prove.

Feather v Keighley (1953)

The contract included a clause by which the contractor undertook not to subcontract work without consent. The terms specifically provided that, if the term was breached, the employer could determine the contract or levy damages in the sum of £100. The contractor did subcontract without consent and the employer terminated the contract. It was held that doing so was a breach of the contract, but not repudiatory in nature. Therefore, whilst the employer was entitled to determine pursuant to the clause, he could not also claim for the additional cost of the replacement contractor.

Sutcliffe v Chippendale and Edmondson (1971)

The defendant prepared a design for the claimant, who was proposing to have a house built. In June 1963 tenders had been invited, and the lowest accepted. Work started in July

1963. The completion date was 31 January 1964. Soon after work commenced the plaintiff had started to express his concern at what he regarded as slow progress. Completion dates slipped by. By mid-May 1964 the house was still not complete and it was apparent that there were numerous defects. The claimant formed the view that the contractors lacked the necessary foreman supervision to carry out the work expeditiously or adequately and dismissed them because they displayed lack of competence or ability to complete the work. The claimant was unable to recover the cost of remedial works from the original contractors who became involvent. Recovery from the architect depended, among other things, upon the claimant's right to determine the contract. The Court considered that the whole combination of circumstances that then existed justified the claimant in ordering the contractors off the site. The Court referred to the contractors' manifest inability to comply with the completion date requirements, the nature and number of complaints from subcontractors, the fact that the quality of work was deteriorating and the number of defects was multiplying, many of which he had tried unsuccessfully to have put right. These all pointed to the conclusion that the contractors had neither the ability, competence or the will by this time to complete the work in the matter required by the contract.

J M Hill v London Borough of Camden (1980)

The facts have been set out above. The claimant contractors' reduction in their labour and plant at the site, whilst amounting to a failure to proceed 'regularly and diligently', was insufficient to amount to repudiation. The claimant did not purport to leave the site and their subsequent conduct indicated that they intended to treat the contract as subsisting.

Sheffield v Conrad (1987)

The claimant was a builder, and the defendant the owner of a small bungalow, which was to be converted into a two-storey house. Work began in May 1982. The defendant believed that progress was slow and by November 1982 instructed the claimant to leave site. After termination, it was discovered that there was a design defect in the cantilevered floor. The official referee found that the reaction of the builder to the discovery of the defect, post-termination, was unsatisfactory and the explanations he put forward at the time, 'quite untenable'. It was argued on behalf of the defendant that in justifying the termination, it is possible to rely upon the conduct of the claimant post-termination, given that the reaction was such that it would (had it happened pre-termination) of itself have destroyed all confidence of the employer in the future so far as the builder was concerned. This argument was rejected. It was possible to take into account breaches as at the date of termination that may not have been known about, but this of itself was insufficient. The defect in the cantilever floor was not of sufficient magnitude to be a breach that went to the root of the contract.

Rice v Great Yarmouth Borough Council (2000)

In a claim concerning an alleged repudiatory breach of a maintenance contract, Lady Justice Hale in the Court of Appeal noted the parallels with building contracts, 'in the number and variety of the obligations involved and the varying gravity of the breaches which may be committed, some of which may be remediable and some not.' The court below had been correct to ask itself whether the cumulative breaches would continue to deliver a substandard performance. Thus, the concept of a contractor's work containing a sufficient extent of defects to warrant the grant of an immediate remedy – rather than waiting to the date for completion – was established as relevant.

IJS Contractors Ltd v Dew Construction Ltd (2000)

The claimant sub-subcontractor was employed by the defendant subcontractor to carry out works to various railway stations for the defendant. There was no written contract, although it was common ground between the parties that the carrying-out of the work was to be governed by stringent safety requirements. Three employees of the claimant were discovered by the main contractor (i.e. the employer of the defendant) to have smoked marijuana during a break. The claimant dismissed the three employees, together with one other employee and a supervisor, and wrote to the defendant stating that they intended to seek prosecution of the individuals. The court at first instance found that the employees' conduct put the claimant in repudiatory breach of its contract with the defendant; this finding was reversed by the Court of Appeal on the basis that the single breach of an implied term to ensure employees would abide by the safety handbook was not so serious a breach of the contract as to entitle the defendant to bring the contract to an end forthwith.

Adkin v Brown (2002)

In this New Zealand case, it was held that an employer was not permitted to terminate for breach of an essential stipulation as to structural safety, as the defects in question could have been remedied and completed for a relatively small sum.

Shawton Engineering Ltd v DGP Ltd (2006)

The action concerned the provision of design drawings by the defendant for the engineering and manufacture of box encapsulation plant for the storage of nuclear waste. So far as the quality of DGP's drawings was concerned, the Court was satisfied that many of the drawings contained errors, including a number of errors which a reasonably competent engineer would not have put forward. However, on the basis that the errors were in general corrected by DGP, the Court considered that the existence of errors went essentially to the question of delay rather than breach of contract of itself. They were insufficient to give the claimant the right to terminate the contract.

Index

additional payment claims *see also* variation claims
   ICE7, 154–156

binding certificates, 42–43
bonuses
   loss of, 167–168

certification, 34
   binding certificates, 42–43
   certificates or approval as condition precedent to payment, 34–35
      ICE conditions, 36–37
      JCT conditions, 35–36
   validity of process, 37–42
claims collation costs, 172
   expert assistance, 173–174
   party's own costs, 174–179
compensation events *see* NEC3
contractual termination *see* termination
contra proferentem rule
   liquidated damages, 71, 75, 77, 80, 117–119

delay claims *see also* loss and expense claims
   global, 62
disruption claims *see* loss and expense claims

entire contract, 1
   complete performance, 3
   substantial performance, 3, 4
exceptionally inclement weather, 72
expense claims *see* loss and expense claims

expert delay/disruption evidence
   delay claims, 184–185
   disruption claims
      activity-specific claims, 186
      'measured mile' claims, 186–187
extensions of time, 61–62
   concurrent delay, 110–113
   delay and determination – time of the essence, 106–110
   entitlement, establishing, 66–82
   liquidated damages, 138
   ownership of float, 113
      position under JCT, 113–114
      position under NEC3, 115
   standard form contracts, 82
      Design and Build Contract (DB) *see* JCT Design and Build Contract 2005
      ICE (7th edition) *see* ICE Form of Contract (7th edition)
      Intermediate Form (IC/ICD), 84–87
      Minor Works (MW/MWD), 83–84
      NEC3 *see* NEC3
      Standard Building Contract (SBQ) *see* JCT Standard Building Contract With Quantities 2005

finance charges
   recovery, 166–167
float

ownership, 113
  position under JCT, 113–114
  position under NEC3, 115

GC/Works/1 (edition 3), 130
General Conditions of Contract and Forms of Tender, Agreement and Bond for use in connection with Works of Civil Engineering Construction (2nd edition), 116
global claims, 62, 179–183

heads of loss *see* loss and expense claims
Housing Grants, Construction and Regeneration Act (HGCRA) 1996
  entitlement to stage payments (s. 109), 6–7, 26
  payment provisions (s. 109–113), 26
  withholding notices (s. 111), 27–32
Hudson's Building Contracts (4th edition), 53

ICE Conditions of Contract (4th edition), 53
ICE Conditions of Contract (5th edition), 11, 36, 190
ICE Conditions of Contract (6th edition), 36–37
ICE Form of Contract (7th edition), 55–58, 149, 190
  additional payments, 154–156
  assessment
    delay, 98
    due date for completion, 98
    extension of time for completion, 97–98
    final determination, 98–99
    interim grant of, 98
  liquidated damages for delay
    damages not a penalty, 143
    intervention of variations etc., 144–145
    limitation, 143
    recovery and reimbursement, 143–144
    substantial completion of whole of works, 141–143
increased overheads *see* loss and expense claims
information
  employers, reliance upon, 49–50
instructions, 48–49

JCT Design and Build Contract 2005, 29, 34, 83
  adjustment of completion date
  fixing completion date, 94–96
  notice by contractor of delay to progress, 93–94
  related definitions and interpretation, 93
  relevant events, 96–97
JCT Intermediate Building Contract 2005, 84–87
JCT Intermediate Form of Building Contract (1984 edition), 192, 193
JCT Minor Works Building Contract 2005, 83–84
JCT Standard Building Contract With Quantities 2005, 82

Index

adjustment of completion date
   fixing completion date, 88–90
   notice by contractor of delay to progress, 88
   related definitions and interpretation, 87
   relevant events, 90–93
loss and expense
   matters materially affecting regular progress, 151–152
   relevant matters, 152–154
partial possession by employer – contractor's consent, 140–141
payment or allowance of liquidated damages, 139–140
JCT Standard Form of Building Contract (1963 edition), 35, 39, 40, 69, 72, 107, 108, 134, 135, 159, 194
JCT Standard Form of Building Contract (1980 edition), 4, 40, 72, 73, 76, 110, 133, 167, 195
JCT Standard Form of Building Contract (1981 edition), 119
JCT Standard Form of Building Contract (1998 edition), 195
JCT Standard Form of Building Contract, Private with Quantities (1963 edition), 15
JCT Standard Form of Building Contract, Private with Quantities (1980 edition), 136, 137
JCT Standard Form of Contract with Contractors Design (1981 edition), 170
JCT Standard Form of Contract with Contractors Design (1998 edition), 24, 31, 129
JCT Standard Form of Management Contract (1987 edition), 190

Keating on Construction Contracts (8th edition), 56, 110, 131, 160, 166
Keating on JCT Contracts, 121

liquidated and ascertained damages (LAD) clauses *see* liquidated damages
liquidated damages, 61, 62, 67, 68, 71, 72, 75, 76, 77, 80, 116–117
   contractual peculiarities, 132
   contractual preconditions to recovery, 136–138
   entries against appendix, 133–134
   extension of time, 138
   ICE7 *see* ICE Form of Contract (7th edition)
   JCT 2005, 139–141
   NEC3, 145–146
   problem of sectional completion, 134–136
   termination, 138–139
   waiver, 139
   contra proferentem rule, 71, 75, 77, 80, 117–119, 134–135
   operable extent of LAD clause, 119–121
   penalty clauses, 124–132

prevention principle, 67, 76, 77, 81
   operation, 121–124
loss and expense claims, 147
   contractual formalities, 149–151
   expert delay/disruption evidence *see* expert delay/disruption evidence
   global claims, 179–183
   heads of loss, 156
      claims collation costs, 172–179
      disruption costs, 165
      finance charges, 166–167
      increased office overheads, 158–159
      increased site overheads, 156–158
      increase in cost of materials, 159–160
      loss of bonus, 167–168
      loss of profit, 164–165
      other losses, 179
      prolongation costs, 156
      sums paid in settlement of third party claims, 168–172
      wasted management time, 161–165
   ICE7, 154–156
   JCT 2005, 151–154
   NEC3, 154
   overriding principles, 147–149
   SCL Protocol, 183–184
loss of productivity, 165
lump sum contracts, 1–9
   entire contract, 1
      complete performance, 3
      substantial performance, 3, 4

MacGregor on Damages (17th edition), 131
management time
   wasted, 161–165
materials
   increased costs, 159–160

NEC Contract ECC3, 58–60
NEC3, 149
   compensation events, 99–102
   notification, 102–104
   quotations, 104–106
   delay damages X7, 145–146
   float, 115
   loss and expense, 154

office overheads
   increased, 159–160
omission of work, 51–53

payment claims
   Housing Grants, Construction and Regeneration Act 1996 see Housing Grants, Construction and Regeneration Act (HGCRA) 1996
   lump sum contracts, 1–9
   prime cost contract, 12
   quantum meruit, 12–25
   remeasurement contract, 9–11
penalty clauses, 124–132
prevention principle, 67, 76, 77, 81
   operation, 121–124
prime cost contract, 12
profits
   loss of, 166
prolongation costs, 156

quantum meruit, 4, 12–25

remeasurement contract, 9–11

repudiatory breach of contract, 199–202
RIBA Conditions of Engagement, 4, 5
RIBA Standard Form of Building Contract (1963 edition), 166
RICS Conditions of Engagement for Building Surveying Services (1981 edition), 192

SBCC Design Portion with Quantities (September 1997 Revision) Building Contract with Scottish Supplement 1980 (revised, July 1997), 30
site overheads
   increased, 156–158
Society of Construction Law (SCL)
   Delay and Disruption Protocol, 183–184
stage payments
   entitlement, *Housing Grants, Construction and Regeneration Act* 1996, s. 109, 6–7
Supply of Goods and Services Act 1982
   s. 14, 63

termination, 188
   contractual, 188
      compliance with notice provisions, 188–193
      other existing rights, 196–199
      unreasonable or vexatious termination, 193–196
   liquidated damages, 138–139
   repudiatory breach of contract, 199–202
third party claims
   sums paid in settlement of, 168–172
time for completion, 62–66
   extension *see* extensions of time
   reasonable time, 63–66

uneconomic working, 165

variation claims, 44–48
   additional work, conditions precedent to claims, 53–54
      ICE Form of Contract (7th edition), 55–58
      JCT Standard Building Contract With Quantities 2005, 54–55
      NEC Contract ECC3, 58–60
   information provided by employer, reliance upon, 49–50
   instructions, 48–49
   omission of work, 51–53

waiver
   liquidated damages, 139

The *Case in Point* series

The *Case in Point* series is a popular set of concise practical guides to legal issues in land, property and construction. Written for the property professional, they get straight to the key issues in a refreshingly jargon-free style.

Areas covered:

Negligence in Valuation and Surveys
Item code: 6388
Published: December 2002

Party Walls
Item code: 7269
Published: May 2004

Service Charges
Item code: 7272
Published: June 2004

Estate Agency
Item code: 7472
Published: July 2004

Rent Review
Item code: 8531
Published: May 2005

Expert Witness
Item code: 8842
Published: August 2005

Lease Renewal
Item code: 8711
Published: August 2005

VAT in Property and Construction
Item code: 8840
Published: September 2005

Construction Adjudication
Item code: 9040
Published: October 2005

Dilapidations
Item code: 9113
Published: January 2006

Planning Control
Item code: 9391
Published: April 2006

Building Defects
Item code: 9949
Published July 2006

Contract Administration
Item Code: 16419
Published March 2007

If you would like to be kept informed when new *Case in Point* titles are published, please e-mail **rbmarketing@rics.org**

All RICS Books titles can be ordered direct by:

- Telephoning 0870 333 1600

- Online at www.ricsbooks.com

- E-mail mailorder@rics.org